NMAWN

SEX ED
UN CENSORED

By TayloR Puck, M.S., M.Ed

WITHDRAWN

Frederick Fell Publishers, Inc
2131 Hollywood Blvd., Suite 305
Hollywood, FL 33020
www.Fellpub.com
email: Fellpub@aol.com

Frederick Fell Publishers, Inc
2131 Hollywood Blvd., Suite 305
Hollywood, Fl 33020

Printed in the United States of America.

14   13   12   11   10   9   8   7   6   5   4   3   2   1

Library of Congress Cataloging-in-Publication Data

Puck, TayloR.
Sex ed uncensored / by Taylor Puck, M.S., M.Ed.
   pages cm
ISBN 978-0-88391-285-0
1. Sex instruction for teenagers. 2. Sex. I. Title.
HQ35.P85 2014
613.9071'2--dc23

                         2014031232

For information about special discounts for bulk purchases, please contact Frederick Fell Special Sales at business@fellpublishers.com or call 945-455-4243.

Print ISBN: 978-088391-285-0
eBook ISBN: 9780883912867

SEX ED
UN CENSORED

Mind Blowing Sex Sh*t!!!
For Young Adults

TayloR Puck, M.S., M.Ed.
(Based on Dr. Dennis Dailey's *Circles of Sexuality*)

'Waiting until marriage': *Why it ISN'T such a good idea*
Drunkin' hook-ups: *The reality of the aftermath*
Masturbation: *How it will help your future relationships*
Sexual orientation: *Find out your true identity*

ACKNOWLEDGMENTS

I'd like to thank the following people for not having a life and responding to my Facebook queries. That, or perhaps they just love me enough and threw in their thoughts to help make this book as inappropriate as possible: Kate Nordstrom, Enloe, Nick Cronin, Russell Berman, Juliana Rippy, Jojo Atria, Ed, Patrick Robertson, Dillon Hill, Brandyn Bundy, Mike Citarella, Don Citarella, Carrieanne Le'Boeuf, Wes Gruver, Chris, Palmer, Jennifer Jones, Spencer Boone, Darren Brown, Stephen Cruz, John Sargent, Joey Arnold, Shannon Grace, Jesse DiPaolo, Rachel Maulding, Ray Donoto, Margaret Morris, Jordan Heymann, Richie Beckham, Tommy Gavin, Disko, Losey, Sestafiesta, SJ, Joe Arnold, Norris Tilton, Jovan, Scott Thomas, Chris & Kristin, Frank Anderson, Laura, Lena, Dave, Shane, Tony, Tina, David, Jason & Joanna, Carlo, Mozden, Johnna, Ian, Maddy, Maggie & Austin.

I couldn't have done this project without Don Lessne of Frederick Fell Publishers, Inc. Thank you for believing in me, Don! And as for everyone else that has helped during the publishing of this book, thank you Emily Leonard, Tevin Wilson, Chad, Evan, Jacinta and Ken.

To Tom and his Chez Café little elves-you are the perfect substitution. Thank you for being the diversion to my *Starbucks* addiction.

To Lunatic Radio—I love you, you bastards!!

As for the *Sands Hotel*… Thank you Carla, Dee, Rachel, Lorna, Tomas, Blanca, Dr. Von Burbage, Amanda, Sebastian, Fran, Lezlee, Geralyn, Lori, Dave, Shirley, Walter, Troy, Lisa & Michael, Alex, Ben, James, Eren, Jan, Howie, Dave, Steve, Nick, Scottie Williams, Billy Rack, Reese, Don, Al, Bob, Kevin, Jeff and especially David Seitz (and of course, his lovely girlfriend, Brit)—who let me steal all of his stolen material.

I'd like to extend a big thank you to Widener University and it's Human Sexuality program for supporting my writing and giving me amazing training in the human sexuality field. And to the M.D. Science Lab fam (especially Randy, Ralph, and Nico-la).

Happy 101st Year, Grandma! Thank you for all of your love and support. To the rest of my family, I adore every single one of you. Thank you for accompanying me through this journey. To the Schneiders, I am so thankful to have all of you as a part of my life. And to my Ft. Lauderdale family: Dean, Ed, Claudia, Kim, Ron, Melissa, Steven, and all of your little ones—words cannot describe my gratitude and love towards all of you. Tray, Molly, Dawn, Jen, Kelly & Chris, I couldn't have asked for a better group of best friends. Speaking of BFFs, Melissa and Tray— I.O.U. Thank you for letting me live off you literally as well as figuratively. At last, a final thank you to the Muffins and my imaginary boyfriend, Jason Pedroza. Well, I guess we're not so imaginary anymore!

Sexual Health & Reproduction......9
Why Do Girls Have Sperm? 11
One Cell To Rule Them All! 19
And To Think, I Almost Swallowed You 23
Condom Sense......35

Sexual Identity 51
Boys Have A Penis, Girls Have A Vulva 53
What's In Your Closet? 63
Look Guys—Big Titties! 75
"He" Gave Me The Best Orgasm Of My Life! 83

Sensuality 89
Are You Saying I'm Fat?!?! 91
Are You Hungry For More? 103
Show Me Your "O" Face 113
Yes, Master. 123
Mind Fucking 131

Sexualization 139
The Cat 141
What's Your Theme Song? 147
Suck My Dick! It's A Gem! 155
Are U Cumming? 165
Ménage À Paw 171
Who's Your Daddy?!?! 177
Does 'No' Really Mean 'No'? 183

Intimacy 195
Tuesday......197
'In A Relationship 203
The Four Rings 209
Better Get A King! 215

Index 222

Sexual Health and Reproduction

This circle of sexuality revolves around the attitudes, behaviors and facts that our culture has assigned to sexuality. Its major components consist of: Sexual behavior, anatomy & physiology, sexual/reproductive systems, contraception/abortion, and sexually transmitted infections.

WHY DO GIRLS HAVE SPERM?

At the age of 23, I was a biology teacher in a Florida public high school. (I know what you're thinking: *Blonde, mid-twenties, Florida teacher…* The answer to your question is, "NO! I did NOT sleep with any of my students." Sorry, Kids. But I *did* quit my job and start writing sex books, so I guess that's half as exciting.)

Anyway one day, while teaching my students how yeast makes bread rise, I received a random question about yeast infections... Of course... As I tried hard to stay on task, the students kept shouting out irrelevant sex inquiries.

I did my best to ignore them and focus on the process of fermentation, but stopped in mid-sentence and turned to the class when I heard the most unnerving question asked by a quiet student named Ethan.

"Miss Puck," he asked. "Why do girls have sperm?"

As the class laughed at him, I softly and adoringly answered, "Ethan, Sweetie... Girls do not have sperm."

I turned back to the white board and tried once again to focus on the intended lesson. Then, I heard his unsettling, defensive reply being shouted over the roar of laughter which had still not faded. "Yes, they do! Haven't you heard, girls cum too!?!?"

At that moment, it was apparent to me that these kids needed to know more about sex than the leavening agent in bread. I thought to myself, *Maybe if I had just used alcohol fermentation as the example, they would have stayed with me...* But I was brought back to the sex question when I saw the confused and angry look on Ethan's face. What was so disturbing about the whole-wheat thing was that Ethan was a sixteen-year-old BOY, who was the father of a two-year-old, with a second on the way.

America is not a tolerant country when it comes to sexuality. When it comes to education, it is one of the most sexually repressed countries in the world. I would know, considering that I worked in several school systems that did not offer proper sex education classes. This wouldn't have bothered me so much if half of my students weren't pregnant.

Since America places such a stigma on sexuality, our sexual education system fails us. Why? Well, parents ignore talking to their kids about it because they think the schools will tell them what they need to know; and the school systems refuse to teach anything because they don't want to deal with drama from the parents who don't want their kids to know "too much"! You have churches telling kids that if they have sex before marriage, they'll go to hell, and kids' best friends' older brothers explaining that blow jobs aren't really considered sex! What the fuck? No wonder kids are knocking each other up before their high school graduation. They have absolutely no consistent sexual messages being delivered to them.

Why do kids need proper, *comprehensive* sex education? Cause they're having sex! Do cats shit in a box?

Don't get me wrong! I'm all in for abstinence-only programs-*if* you're in elementary school. However, studies show that the only time abstinence-only programs work with young teens is when they have strong religious beliefs. What that means is that students who attend a Catholic/Baptist middle school may be positively affected by an abstinence-only sex education program; but, place that program in a regular, public middle school- Well, you might as well throw those moralistic sex values out the window. And high schools? I don't care what the religious background is! An abstinence-only program is NOT going to work! Let me explain why:

Kids are having sex at earlier ages, because they're bodies are developing at an earlier age, telling these youngsters that biologically, they're ready to fuck! Every fifty years, the average age of menarche (a girl's first period) occurs approximately one year earlier. So, for instance; in the mid-1800s the average age was 16-17 years old. Today, it's around twelve. Currently, the average age for boys to reach puberty is around twelve as well. Well, back in the day, it was normal for a woman and a man to get married around the age of 15 or 16. So, it was easy for them to wait until marriage. Nowadays, if they're smart, they'll hold off on marriage, go to college and you know-live a little! So for those kids, the gap between their sexual maturity and the age of their first marriage widens; therefore, as they enter adulthood and come into their own, holding off on sexual activity for such a long extension of time becomes extremely difficult. Almost impossible!

The result of teaching them to wait until they're married- Well, think of it this way: How would you like it if every time you felt a sexual urge you mindfucked yourself into thinking it was wrong. *Not until you're married…. Not until you're married…. Stop thinking these things!!! Not until you're married….* Your thinking will eventually become warped… But this tour will not be fun. There will be no 311, Pennywise or NOFX. Instead, you'll be rushing to the alter to marry your high school sweetheart; only to find that when the time came for you to actually lose your virginity, you've now been blessed with a sexual dysfunction! *Yay!* Because while you're telling your body (which has been ready to be sexually active for several years now) to finally behave like that porn star that you've been aspiring to be… Well, shocker!!!! It's not going to perform up to par! Classical conditioning, Loves. It's like Pavlov's adorable dogs. Your dick and/or vag has been told for the past some-odd years to deactivate every time they're excited and raring to go! They've been told, "NO! Bad vag!/Down boy!"

while you've subconsciously tried to counteract your natural, bodily functions with thoughts of your naked grandmother or the Sahara Desert. What-you think just because you've signed a legal document, they're going to rise to the occasion or flood up as if the levy has finally been broken down? Yes, Hurricane Katrina made New Orleans wet; but, that wasn't necessarily a good thing... Abstinence-only programs promote a message that is not as ideal as it may seem.

The good news is, we have found an effective form of sexual education! *Comprehensive* sex education! And being "comprehensive" means that it encompasses EVERY aspect of sexuality, including abstinence! So, those people who believe in 'abstinence-only' should be happy; because, students who will be positively affected by this message will be exposed to it. As for students who will not abide by the 'abstinence-only' rules, they will still be exposed to the material, but will also receive the tools that they need to be safe during their chosen sexual escapades! *Well, what if comprehensive sex education makes students want to have sex, since all their doing is hearing about it?*—Fear not, People! Research says that comprehensive sex education DOES NOT instigate sexual activity at an earlier age. So, why not provide everyone with the right information so that they can make their own choices and do so correctly?

Every organism's number one goal in life is to reproduce. We unconsciously desire to spread our seeds and continue our genetic pool. In urban terms: We want to fuck! It's evolution, my dear Friends! So 'abstinence-only' programs are trying to block kids' number one, biological goal in life; which in return, encourages them to jump into a marriage at a young age...

...That makes sense...

Kids, my goal as your guide is to help reduce the stigma of sexuality that America has etched into your brains and help you celebrate it! But before we beam up to the *Enterprise*, please let me point out the obvious. The reason why sex is so taboo in America is because people do it incorrectly... You see, everyone does it. Take a moment and take a snapshot in your head of all of the people "doing it" right now! There are millions of people having sex as you read this sentence. But the question is: How many of them are doing it safely? Well, I don't know the answer to that question, but you can damn-sure bet on the fact that there have been at least one hundred babies that are in the process of being conceived during the time it has taken you to finish this paragraph.

The result of these unprotected bouts of sex? More people. We are taught that the human race is growing at an exponential rate. Why? Because people can't afford to pay their cable bill, so they procreate instead. And we wonder why we have so much poverty... Stop blaming the presidents; at least Obama recommends sex education for grades K-12. That's right! Obama's an advocate for **proper, age-appropriate** sex education from kindergarten on. Get 'em while their young! And I don't mean that in a pedophilic way. I mean it in an educational way. Otherwise... Well, have you ever seen the movie *Idiocracy*? Worst movie EVER! But unfortunately, it's right on target with predicting the intelligence of our future society.

For those of you who believe that the sex education that our country provides "isn't *that* bad", here's a reality check for you: Only twenty-one states require sex education to be taught in schools. Now, this doesn't mean that the other states don't offer sex education; it's just not mandated. (That's less than half of our country...) Thirty-three states mandate HIV education... (This makes sense... Cause HIV education is *really* going to effective without being accompanied with proper sex education...) Only nineteen states require education on condoms or contraception... (Let me repeat that: *NINETEEN!!!!*) It gets worse: Only twelve states require their sex education classes to be medically accurate. *And here's my favorite*... Eleven states require discussion on sexual orientation; but, three of those will not allow any discussion on sexual orientation to be carried out in the classrooms *unless* it reflects sexual orientation in a negative manner. That's right! Good ol' Texas, South Carolina and Alabama…

No offense, Kids… But you're ignorant. Can we blame you?!? Hell no! You haven't had one bit of proper education thrown your way! And, as a result, you are close-minded, judgmental and dumbfounded when it comes to sexuality. What makes matters worse is that at your age, your actions and words affect and mold other people around you. So, you are constantly spreading negative messages on sexuality. "Sex up the butt?!?! EW! Who in their right mind would EVER allow someone to do that?!?!?" YOU… In five years.

So, keep an open mind while you continue to read forth, and embark on this eye-opening sexual journey. While reading this book, you will learn to become more tolerant of everything and everyone when it comes to others' views and expressions on sexuality. Why? Because my job, as a trained sex educator, is to normalize every aspect of sex. And I'm good at what I do! Based off of Dr. Dennis Dailey's *Circles of Sexuality*, this book provides you with a proper comprehensive sex education lesson. Granted, it's quite explicit; but beneath this jaw-dropping, juicy gossip, underlies moral principles. And I promise, as you leave your prejudices behind and read forward, you will be nothing short of entertained.

As a final note: I make my biases obvious, because I am the author of this book… And I can! I also have uncalled humor embedded throughout the book for entertainment purposes, and honestly—I'm not going to ignore the fact that people joke inappropriately. It doesn't mean that I'm racist, or a sellout—it just means I'm fucking funny! As for my use of foul language, I can't help that I curse like a sailor. Well, I guess I can… But I don't care enough to censor my language. So, my advice to those of you who are bothered by it, just change all of my "fuck"s to "puck"s. That way, my writing will seem much less offensive, and you'll be subliminally programming yourself to use my name in inappropriate situations.

REFERENCES:

Avert.org. (n.d.). Abstinence and sex education. Retrieved from ttp://www.avert.org/abstinence.htm

Bearman, P. & Brucknew, H. (2001). Promising the future: Virginity pledges and first intercourse. *American Journal of Sociology*, 106(4): 859-912.

Buss, D. M. (1989). Sex differences in human mate preferences: Evolutionary hypotheses tested in 37 cultures. *Behavioral and Brain Sciences*, 12, 1-49.

Education-Portal.com. (2007, July 25). The fight over sex education in public schools. Retrieved from http://educationportal.com/articles/The_ Fight_Over_Sex_Education_in_Public_Schools.html

Guttmacher Institute. (2012, September 10). *State policies in brief: Sex and HIV education.* Retrieved from https://www.guttmacher.org/ statecenter/spibs/spib_SE.pdf

Judge, M. & Koplovitz, E. (Producers), & Judge, M. (Director). (2006). *Idiocracy* [Motion picture]. United States: Twentieth Century Fox Film Corporation.

McHenry, D. & Jackson, G. (Producers), & Van Peebles, M. (Director). (1991). *New Jack City* [Motion picture]. United States: Warner Bros. Pictures.

Rees, M. (1995). The age of menarche. *OBGYN*, 4, 2-4.

Taflinger, R. F. (1996). *Biological Basis of Sex Appeal.* Retrieved from http://public.wsu.edu/~taflinge/biosex1.html

ONE CELL TO RULE THEM ALL!

Have you ever seen or read *The Lord of the Rings: The Two Towers* book or movie? You know the battle of Helm's Deep, when the Orcs breach the fortress? Well, that's kind of similar to the way you were born! Except instead of Orcs, there were sperm. Around 300,000,000 to be exact… About the same as a rabbit. But if you're a pig… Then, it's more like 8,000,000,000! In any case they're attempting to break down a wall!

So, as you may already know from your Biology class, that when the most fit sperm breaks into the egg, it creates a zygote (a fertilized egg). Five days later, it develops into a blastocyst, which turns into an embryo, which turns into a fetus, which is born as YOU! But the growth doesn't stop there. Your mind and body continues to grow from the moment you're a zygote to the moment you're a corpse. Yes, even before you are born your body undergoes sexual changes. See? And that's why even if you're not having sex, you're still considered a sexual being.

Did you know that before you exit the womb you've probably masturbated, have experienced an erection or vaginal lubrication, and possibly even contracted an STI?!? That's the worst way to get one. Talk about being in the wrong womb at the wrong time! But like I wrote before, you're a sexual being. You are the result of sex and for many of you, you'll die while having sex!

When you're born the sexual milestones begin. Genital

stimulation occurs right away! In some cultures, it's actually acceptable to rub your child's genitals to quiet them down. Just like in Alabama culture, it's acceptable to rub rum on your child's gums. But whether it's from a little rub and tug or a tasty bourbon, a baby can actually reach orgasm before the age of three! But, don't expect a baby boy in his terrible two stage to start slinging yogurt at you. The semen and sperm don't appear until the onset of puberty.

Not only is a toddler sexually experienced enough to orgasm, but a young child under the age of five also undergoes a series of psycho-social and gender role milestones. They determine a strong sense of self as a male or female. In doing this, they usually attempt to be the other sex. Ever hear of "dress up"? It's the most popular cross-dressing game for toddlers.

The innocence fades away pretty much after the age of five, and it's replaced with a dirty mind with an unlimited warranty. Children between the ages of six and nine start asking a lot of sex questions. And get this! They actually find pleasure in hearing sexual jokes! Do they actually *get* all of the punch lines? Probably not, but they *get* the inappropriate behavior. Body image issues start occurring at this age, and sexual orientations "supposedly" develop at this time. (Although that's arguable, since people claim that they've "always known".) Oh, did I mention that those first few stragglers of pubic hair start growing in? Ew…

Crushes supposedly develop around the double digits; although, I'm debating this one, considering I can name at least ten different boys I was crushing on before the age of ten. Sexual, erotic, romantic fantasies also begin at this stage. (That one I will agree with. I don't remember visualizing bondage scenes with my first grade crush… He did however pee on me. But I think that was accidental, not meant for erotic purposes…)

Then puberty begins! Awkwardness galore! If you didn't have body issues developing while you were in elementary school, you have them now. Acne, growth spurts, gynecomastia (boob growth in men), breast development in women, menarche, and wet dreams (here come the semen and sperm)! Puberty is a lot like boot camp! It's miserable, and it's preparing you for war! Again, I refer to sex as war, but it kind of is! Your body is preparing you to conquer!

It is at the onset of puberty (if not before) when kids start looking for sexual information. They're also able to get pregnant; so for those people who don't believe in providing proper sex education to middle schoolers-you're out of your fucking mind!

During the teen years, most kids become sexually active and take part in intimate relationships. Once a boy reaches the age of 18, his orgasms become more intense. However, a woman's orgasm intensity increases later in life (around her thirties). Luckily, by then men are able to last longer and hopefully know where the clitoris is!

You may think that the milestones stop here, but if so, you're far from accurate. We are all aware of the loss of testosterone in men, and the loss of vaginal lubrication in women. But don't think for a second that just because people age they're having sex less. Your grandparents? Doin' it! Possibly right now-as you read this statement! Sorry to put the idea into your head... But it's true! Don't know what to get your widowed grandmother for her birthday? Bet she's in need of a new vibrator! Most women are...

The sexuality of a person changes nonstop through one's timeline, and is dependent on a multitude of components. Whether it's a new car giving a guy a boost of confidence, or sleep deprivation decreases one's overall drive, the overall sense of wellbeing affects one's sexuality. Examples like getting married, dealing with a death, taking medicine, losing weight, a new job, arthritis, a car accident, or simply a new crush will alter one's sexuality. So next time your lover goes through a rough patch, be patient and don't take offense if they're not in the mood.

When does one finally reach a point when they are mentally and physically ready to establish a serious relationship? When does one finally learn to honestly communicate with others? When does one reach a point where they are truly satisfied with their own bodies? Who the hell knows? It maybe happens at a young age, or maybe never. And even if they do reach that point in their lives, there is a chance that they lose that sense of sexuality as they age.

As you read further into this book, you will be able to untangle the complexity of the word "sexuality". It is not all about X-rated sex. Yes, sexuality refers to our bodies during puberty, and the first time we 'do it'; but, it also refers to our emotions, spiritual growth, intellect, and how we see others and ourselves as sexual beings. It is everything about us as well as the foundation of every relationship we encounter throughout our lives.

REFERENCES:

Heasley, R. & Crane, B. (Eds.). (2003). *Sexual Lives A Reader on the Theories and Realities of Human Sexualities.* New York: McGraw-Hill Higher.

Meizner, I. (1987). Sonographic observation of in utero fetal "masturbation". *Journal of Ultrasound in Medicine,* 6(2), 111.

Olson, E. (2013). Why are 250 million sperm cells released during sex? Retrieved from http://www.livescience.com/32437-why-are-250-million-sperm-cells-released-during-sex.html

Osborn, B., Jackson, P., Walsh, F. (Producers), & Jackson, P. (Director). (18 July 2002). *The Lord of the Rings: The Two Towers* [Motion picture]. Los Angeles: New Line Cinema.

WebMD. (2013). Sex and aging. Retrieved from http://www.webmd.com/healthy-aging/guide/sex-aging

AND TO THINK, I ALMOST SWALLOWED YOU

My goal, as TayloR Puck (TRP), is to extinguish teenage pregnancies. Now, I am not telling you to do anything against your God's(s') or parents' wishes; but, I am here to provide you with medically accurate information so when the time comes that you are sexually active and need to make certain decisions, you are capable of making healthy choices.

For those of you who are already teenage parents, congratulations! I commend and support you! God knows, I would have never been able to take on that challenge at such an young age. And I hope that you have the financial and emotional support in order to give your child the life they deserve. As for you and any other teen, please take the following information in stride, and hold off on having any more children until you've matured a bit more. Take the next five to ten years and focus on your life. Now is the time to make yourself your number one priority. Learn how to be safe so you can kick back, go to college, progress educationally as well as mentally and have fun!

The following information is to provide you with a list of birth control and contraception options. When we talk about "birth control" we are discussing preventing birth from taking place. Methods of birth control are anything that causes the fertilized egg from implanting itself on the uterine wall. It doesn't necessarily

STOP the egg from getting fertilized. So, if you tell people that your preferred way of birth control is an abortion, depending on your delivery, you may be funny. But if you're serious, you're a fucking waste of space. Please die off quickly so we can make room for less ignorant people on the planet. As for contraception, these prevention methods keep the egg and sperm from ever coming face-to-face. (I don't know what's more sad: Using contraception and never letting the princess ever meet her prince, or using birth control and having the dragon eat both of them, killing them simultaneously…we should probably focus on a happier fairy-tale ending… At least you don't end up with a baby!!)

Please note: I do not list any side effects or disadvantages to any of the options below. This is because 1) I am not a medical doctor. Any form of birth control that you are interested in using must be decided upon by you, your partner, your medical doctor and possibly your parents. And 2) I don't want to focus on the negatives of any of the following. To me, they're all fucking awesome because they prevent you from getting pregnant! *Sweet…* But for entertainment and educational purposes, I have rated all of them with the 'TayloR Puck Rating (TRPR) System' to show you their level of effectiveness. Do not confuse the TayloR Puck Ratings as my personal preferences; the rating system is purely based on the statistical data of their effectiveness **as birth control and/or contraception**, NOT as a prevention method against STIs.

Abstinence: Abstinence is the best way to ensure keeping your number a "1" on line "A" of your W-4 form, but it's definitely the hardest. If I could, I would advise every youngster to 'Remember Jesus-and not get nailed'! But no matter how many fundies are advocating "Abstinence-Only" education, it's just not that practical. Once kids reach puberty, they are biologically ready to have sex. Mentally, on the other hand is different for everyone. What advice work for you? I don't fucking know! But here's a little sextra advice:

Masturbate! A LOT! By yourself and mutually with your partner. Because most people don't experience the most out of sex until they become fully sexual with themselves. And that learning process is a fucking fun journey between you, yourself, and anyone else who you allow to accompany you. Once **you** fully discover your own body sexually, you'll then be prepared to allow someone else to discover yours. So hold off on the whole sex crap until you're ready… Mentally AND physically… And only you can be the true judge of that.

Even though to some, abstinence is the least fun, it is 100% effective. Since this is the case, it gets the highest grade on the TayloR Puck Scale:

TRPR: A+

The Pill: The most popular form of contraception is the pill. The pill is taken every day for twenty or twenty-one days and when stopped; the menstruation is triggered to begin. During the final week, there are "sugar" pills for the female to continuously take to help her stay on track, or she can just take the week off and be pill-free! The pill contains synthetic estrogen and/or progesterone, which regulates egg production and the menstrual cycle. The pill actually fools the body into thinking that it's pregnant by altering the hormone balance. This in turn prevents ovulation, so the egg is never released. A period still happens though, because the lining of womb sheds during the "sugar week" when it's not receiving the additional hormones.

For those of you on the pill who suffer from extreme mood swings, ask your doctor for another prescription. There are plenty of different choices. And even though this pill is the one pill your man won't mind you on, he doesn't deserve to deal with your unnecessary Pissy Mood Syndrome (PMS).

TRPR: A

The Depo: This injectable contraceptive is a progestin-only method that is effective immediately. The *Depo-Provera* (DMPA) consists of four, tiny injections a year and produces a pregnant-free woman during every three month interval. (Dude, if I were a parent of a teenage girl, I would SO put her on this instantaneously, JUST to prevent an eighteen year headache for all of us.)

TRPR: A

The Patch: *Ortho Evra* is a form of birth control that releases synthetic estrogen and progestin to protect against pregnancy. Just like a nicotine patch, this patch can be stickered to your lower abdomen, your ass, your arm (like a classy tattoo) or the upper torso. Every seven days the woman must remove and replace the patch, which may seem annoying, but it's a lot less annoying than remembering to take a pill at the same time every day. During the patch-free week, the woman menstruates… You'd think this is the week she would need a band-aid.

TRPR: A

The NuvaRing: The *NuvaRing* is the last form of hormonal birth control. This vaginal ring releases synthetic estrogen and progestin, which once again, prevents ovulation. The *NuvaRing* gets tossed up the vag every 28 days and remains up there for only 21. The last week is ring free! 95% of women say they have no problem with the insertion of the *NuvaRing*, which would make chances of conquering the *NuvaRing* much more likely than conquering the game of ring toss. (Cause I don't know about you, but I don't care how many glass bottles are at that carnival's ring toss game—those little red rings DON'T FUCKING FIT, DAMN-IT!)

TRPR: A

The Condom: I guess I have to give the proper definition of a condom here… (But I'm pretty sure that the chances that the reader knows what a "condom" is are higher than them knowing what a "sheath" is.) Well, a condom is a sheath that fits over the penis that is form of barrier birth control. A sheath (for those of you who don't know) is a cover. This thin material is usually made out of latex, polyurethane, or processed animal tissue lambskin.

Telling your doctor that the condom broke is like telling your teacher that your dog ate your homework. Either way, you end up looking like a dumb-ass. A condom is not 100% effective, but it is the best protection method when it comes to both pregnancy and STIs. So use condom sense… Correctly… Dumbass…

TRPR: A

The Female Condom: The female condom is a loose-fitting polyurethane sheath that gets placed up the vag. It has a circular shape on top, which covers the entrance of the cervix and a circular opening for the penis or any other phallic object to enter safely.

*Just a condom side note here: Multiple condoms should never be used simultaneously. I'm referring to two regular, male condoms, or a female and male condom. The extra rubbing causes friction which will deteriorate the materials.

TRPR: B +

The Diaphragm: Just like the female condom, the diaphragm covers the opening of the cervix. It is a little, rubber cup that looks like a little hat. It is stuffed up into the vagina and blocks the sperm en route, creating a barrier between the vaginal canal and the uterus. Women must be measured by a medical practitioner in order to get the right sized diaphragm. And they should be measured at different points throughout their sexual lives; considering women change sizes, especially after pregnancy. When inserted, it provides protection for up to six hours. After intercourse, the woman should leave it in place for another six hours. If sex is repeated, a dosage of spermicide is encouraged. When the woman wants to remove the diaphragm, she needs to insert her finger up into her vag, hook the rim of the diaphragm, and dislodge!

Diaphragms are usually used with spermacides or jellies; although, if you put too much icing on it, it may eventually look like a *Snowball* cake. If this is the case, avoid eating it. Diaphragms are not edible. And if you did attempt a nibble, it would probably do an excellent job acting like a barrier while laying on your pharynx, which would in turn, lead to your untimely death.

TRPR: B

The Cervical Cap: Just like the diaphragm, the cervical cap (another hat-looking device) lays snugly over the cervix, coincides with spermacide, and must remain in place after intercourse for six hours. Women must also be measured when choosing this barrier method, because a perfect fit is extremely important. The major differences between the cervical cap and the diaphragm are that the cervical cap is smaller, has a deeper cup, and must be placed inside eight hours ahead of time, as well as be left on longer.

TRPR: B-

The Sponge: Luckily people don't need to run off like Elaine from *Seinfeld*, because the sponge is back! Although the reality is that it's not used as much as it was in the past. It kind of looks like soap on a rope. It's plastic and contains spermicide. Like the diaphragm and cervical cup, it can be left inside of the uterus for up to 24 hours.

TRPR: B-

Spermacides: A spermacide is a toxic lube that kills sperm. It is not recommended to be used alone; but, contraceptive foam, contraceptive film, creams, jellies, and other vaginal suppositories can be a perfect additive to create a great birth control/contraception combination for you!

A downfall to repeated spermicidal use is that it wears down the vaginal lining, which could theoretically make women more susceptible to contracting HIV.

TRPR: C

IUD: This intrauterine device is inserted into the uterus, and hangs out through the cervical os (opening). These little "T"s lay snuggly in the uterus, but create a hostile environment. Some are made of copper, which is toxic to sperm; and others release the hormone progestin, which makes the cervical mucus thicker. The mucus then acts like the *Blog* and prevents the sperm from reaching the yellow brick tube. (No matter what, it's a horror movie for these little rascals...) Anyway, this form of birth control can remain inside of a woman for 5-12 years.

In case you were wondering, an IUD is NOT an abortifacient, a device that causes abortions. It just prevents the fertilization act from ever occurring.

TRPR: A

Fertility Awareness-Based Methods: The fertility awareness-based (FAB) methods, otherwise known as "family planning" are great methods to use when you're trying to conceive. Unfortunately, not so much when you're trying NOT to conceive. These include the calendar method, the basal body temperature method and the ovulation method. All three methods are favorable to women because each one, used either separately or combined, teaches them to learn about their bodies, track their ovulation, and become more intuitive with their reproductive system.

The calendar (rhythm) method involves tracking the female's

menstrual history. IF she has a regular period, she is able to figure out the regular period (Get it?!?) of ovulation. During ovulation, the egg is ONLY available to become fertilized for one to two days, so the plan is for her to abstain from sex during her these couple of days or use other forms of birth control.

The reason why this is an extremely faulty method is because NORMAL ovulation occurs fourteen days before menstruation... Give or take two to four days... That's only for someone who gets their unaltered period on the exact due date of every month. Notice how it's already unreliable because there's an extra give and take period of two to four days... In addition, sperm can frolic around in a vagina for up to four days... Some say even more... Therefore, if you're expecting to ovulate on the 10th, you need to avoid having sex between the 10th and the 12th... But don't forget those two to four days... So, make that the 6th through the 16th... But then again, sperm can AT LEAST live up to four days... Maybe more... So, we'll say five to be safe. So extend that ovulation phase from the 1st through the 16th. That's half the month right there!

I know what you're thinking... We'll at least now I know that I can have unprotected sex before, during and after my period. Unfortunately, a female can ovulate at any time; and that includes during her bleeding frenzy. It really depends on how steady your cycle is; and even then, you never know. One major factor that fucks up a female's menstrual cycle is stress. Are you ever NOT stressed? I wouldn't take that chance.

The second FAB method is the basal body temperature (BBT) method. Everyone has a body temperature. A woman's temperature drops during menstruation and the week after. Before ovulation it drops a tad, and then it has a sharp rise. A woman using this method must take her temperature every day for six to twelve months in order for it to work somewhat effectively. The flaw in this technique is that we're talking a few tenths of a degree difference. If you are coming down with something or your temperature is off for another reason, it's not a reliable source to tell you when that little egg is or is not on its way. Another downside, is math. I don't know about you, but I don't DO math. And creating little girds with X and Y axes is the last thing I want to do each morning before my cup of coffee.

Finally, the ovulation method is extra icky! It requires the woman to play with her cervical mucus! *Fun!!* Usually after menstruation women receive cloudy, white discharge. Then, for a couple of days a stretchy, elastic mucus appears. It kind of looks like sticky, uncooked egg whites. *Yum!!* This is the indication that ovulation is occurring. The problem with this method is that there are plenty of factors that can affect your cervical mucus: sexual arousal, food allergies, antibiotics, vitamins, vaginal infections, weight gain and delayed ovulation (stress). Sounds iffy to me. We'll give all three an "F" to play it safe.

TRPR: F

Plan B: The morning-after-pill is a form of emergency contraception (EC) is a **back-up** plan in case someone makes a sexual mistake. And let's face it: Mistakes happen! It contains levonorgestrel, which is found in most birth control pills, and is more effective—the sooner you take it. What does that mean!?!?! If the condom breaks, or if you wake up naked and drunk with a sore crotch, run to your pharmacy IMMEDIATELY and buy it! Because luckily, our country has made one smart decision regarding sexual education and now allows teens (17 and over) to purchase this VERY necessary necessity when necessary.

TRPR: B+

Abortion: Unless ordered by your doctor for medical purposes, an abortion is a back-up plan to the back-up plan. But let's face it: If you intellectually already used a back-up plan, you wouldn't be finding yourself in this position.

There are different types of abortions that are available at different trimesters, but the two major ones that women usually undergo during the first trimester are a medical or surgical abortion.

The medical abortion, is when a drug (usually Mifepristone, commonly known as RU-486, or the "abortion pill") is given orally or injected into the patient, followed by Misopostol tablets, which the patient is instructed to take orally up stick up the vag.

The surgical abortion is much more invasive. The most popular in the United States is the vacuum aspiration, or the suction curettage, which uses local anesthesia. This fifteen minute performance is done after the conceptus, placenta, and endometrial tissue have been vacuumed out of the uterus.

There are other forms of surgical abortion, but whether you're submitting yourself for a vacuum aspiration, dialation and evacuation or hysterectomy, they all sound pretty fucking miserable… AND expensive for that matter. I bet people sitting in that waiting room wish that they just bought the fifty dollar Plan B the day after, instead of 'letting it ride'.

TRPR: A+

Withdraw: The withdrawal, or pulling out method, is when the man pulls his dick out before he cums. It has been rumored that this "contraception" method is 87% effective. This may seem high, but here's the deal. No matter how good a guy is at predicting the time of his blow, he cannot feel the slight precum that seeps out of him, and there are still millions of sperm being leaked at that moment in time. Therefore, if a guy is using the pull-out method at the right time of ovulation, that couple is fucked… Literally. Which is why I'm overriding the "87% effectiveness rate of this birth control method and replacing it with an "F".

Just like spermicidal usage, this is another technique that is an excellent addition to another form of birth control/ contraception. Pulling out and ejaculating all over your partner is always fun for both parties. Just make sure she's wearing some shades. Getting shot in the eye sure as hell stings… And stay away from the hair… It's just a disaster getting that shit out.

TRPR: F

The Tying of the Tubes: One of the most popular tubal ligations is a laparoscopy. During this procedure, the woman's abdomen is inflated with gas so the doctor can see the organs clearly. Then, the doctor goes in through the belly-button with the laparoscope, a lens with x-ray vision, followed with tiny forceps that have heat-vision! The fallopian tubes are cauterized and the left-over tube ends are pinched off with tiny clips. Women who choose this method should not want any more children because it is not considered a reversible process; although, it is rumored that the procedure has no effect on Superman's super sperm.

TRPR: A+

Vasectomy: A vasectomy is when a man gets his vas deferens surgically cut so the sperm have no pathway to the penis. Like the tubal ligation procedure, this surgery is non-reversible. During this minor surgery, the doctor makes an incision in the scrotum, lifts each vas deferens, cuts them and ties them. Since there is still sperm left in the penile area, it may take up to 20 ejaculations (some say more) to get rid of each and every one of those little fuckers. So, start counting down! Twenty-two cho-king chic-kens on the wall, twenty-two cho-king chic-kens. Beat one off, polish the knob, twenty-one cho-king chic-kens on the wall!

Although they claim this surgery is only 99.9% effective, because there has been a report that the vas deferens have grown back together-this is bull shit. If the surgery is done correctly, it is 100% effective ending this lovely chapter with another A+!

TRPR: A+

REFERENCES:

American Pregnancy Association. (2011). Medical abortion procedures. Retrieved from http://www.americanpregnancy.org/unplannedpregnancy/medicalabortions.html

Mehlman, P. (Writer) & Ackerman, A. (Director). (December 7, 1995). The Sponge. In Castle Rock Entertainment, *Seinfeld*. United States: NBC.

Natural Fertility Breakthrough. (2011). The little known factors that affect your cervical mucus and your chances of getting pregnant fast. Retrieved from http://naturalfertilitybreakthrough.com/articles/the-little-known-factors-that-affect-your-cervical-mucus-and-your-chances-of-getting-pregnant-fast/

Planned Parenthood. (2012). Birth control sponge (Today sponge). Retrieved from http://www.plannedparenthood.org/health-topics/birth-control/birth-control-sponge-today-sponge-4224.htm

Planned Parenthood. (2012). Withdrawal (Pullout method). Retrieved from http://www.plannedparenthood.org/health-topics/birth-control/withdrawal-pull-out-method-4218.htm

Strong, B., Yarber, W.L., Sayad, B.W., & DeVault, C. (2008). *Human Sexuality: Diversity in Contemporary America* (6th ed.). Boston: McGraw Hill.

Vasectomy.com. (2012). Top 10 vasectomy questions and answers. Retrieved from http://www.vasectomy.com/articledetail.asp?siteid=V&ArticleId=4

WebMD. (2012). Birth control and the IUD (Intrauterine device). Retrieved from http://www.webmd.com/sex/birth-control/iud-intrauterine-device

Weiner, J. (2012). Goodreads. Retrieved from http://www.goodreads.com/quotes/tag/safe-sex

Yourcontraception.com. (2012). Difference between cervical cap and diaphragm. Retrieved from http://www.yourcontraception.com/birth-control-methods/vaginal-contraception/difference-between-cervical-cap-and-diaphragm.html

CONDOM SENSE

Is oral sex actually considered sex? The correct answer is, "Yes". TayloR Puck's answer is: "I don't give a shit! You can still catch an STI from it! So, use a fucking condom!"

First things first: Please stop saying "STD"! It's politically incorrect! They are not all considered diseases! Yes, this term is still used... But it shouldn't be! (For those of you dumbasses out there that need further clarification, we are discussing "Sexually Transmitted Infections" verses "Sexually Transmitted Diseases".) "Infection" is a more broad term that describes a condition that can hopefully be cured; whereas, "disease" describes something that has already upgraded to a detrimental stage. Since most of them can be cured/treated, we'd like to wishfully hope it's an infection, rather than a disease. Consider it a positive way of looking at venereal "diseases".

Thankfully, most condom companies have had the decent courtesy to update their packaging to the correct terminology; therefore, if you read the back and it still says the acronym "STD" you can assume it's expired and the condom shouldn't be used anyway. But then again, you already checked the expiration date and would have known that anyway... Right?

Are condoms 100% effective? No. But they're the next best thing to abstinence. And if you are mature enough to have sex with another mature and willing partner, I sure as hell hope that you're **smart** enough to take the correct safety precautions. And what that means is to not only use a condom, but to use it correctly; as well as get tested for STIs on a regular basis.

How to Use a Condom
By TayloR Puck, M.S., M.Ed.

Step #1: Look at the expiration date and make sure it's not out of date.

Step #2: Do the pillow test-squeeze the package to make sure no air escapes.

Step #3: Tear (not rip) open the condom carefully.

Step #4: Clearly differentiate between the inside and the outside of the condom.

Step #5: Place the condom correctly on the penis.

Step #6: Pinch the reservoir tip.

Step #7: Unroll.

Step #8: Roll... Around in the hay.

P.S. Don't forget to hold the condom on the penis while withdrawing. Because you know how after you cum, you just want to lay there and hold each other for a while? Well, Dude... Your dick shrinks during this cuddle session. And sometimes if you don't pull out correctly, the condom is left alone inside-rendering your conscientious effort to use birth control completely pointless.

Please take note that a major problem that is not stressed enough when it comes to condom usage is Step #3. This step reduces the flip flaw. The flip flaw is when a guy stupidly puts a condom on his dick upside down, tries to unroll it and realizes he put it on incorrectly. This is usually followed by the boy releasing a goofy laugh as he flips the condom on correctly, which allows him to hastily roll the rubber down. Well, what this ass-clown doesn't know is that when the inside of the condom was lying on the tip of his penis, a tiny dollop of precum leaked into it. Therefore, when he flipped the condom and stuck his dick into his woman, guess what was the first thing to be shot up inside of her? *Millions* of his milky, little seedlings!

Now that you know how to use a condom CORRECTLY, let's discuss dental dams, shall we? I wouldn't suggest using these mini blankets while kissing; although, it *could* prevent you from catching cooties from your kissing buddy. Instead, it is recommended to use these little blankies when orally pleasuring your partner's anus or vaginal area. You just lay the latex sheath over the area, and lick away! (If you're allergic to latex, just like condoms, dental dams are made of other materials. Don't be lazy and make that your excuse to why you aren't playing it safe.) And if you choose to play it safe, don't be a fucktard and always remember to use the same side up against the body. Please. If you're going to be smart enough to take safety precautions, take them correctly.

Finally, the safety lesson is close to being over; but, here is one last demand: YOU MUST get tested on a regular basis! I don't care if you've been in a monogamous relationship with a squeaky clean person for five years. People cheat because it's easier than studying! Yes, if you're in a monogamous relationship you don't have to get tested as regularly as someone who sleeps around more than a couch surfer; but, it still should be done. As for you single, sexually active people who are sloring around all over the place, you should aim for every three months. The window is always open in your case, so make it a routine priority.

It's very important that when you go to your personal physician or local clinic, you ask what STIs they can and will test for. If you go in asking to be generally tested for STIs, they'll take some blood and ask you to pee in a cup. A couple of days later, they'll call you in and ask that you return to the office to pick up the results. (They'll always ask that you to physically return for a consultation, even if your results are negative. It's against protocol for them to deliver results over the phone, so don't even bother asking.) If you don't specify ahead of time, you may be upset with the half-ass results chart, because most locations only offer testing for the main ones, i.e., HIV, Gonorrhea, Chlamydia, and Herpes. There will probably be no Hepatitis C and HPV (considering you need a swab for this one). So, when you order your tests, be specific and order the ones you want—ALL OF THEM!

Funny, how you're taught that if you have sex before you get married, you're going to get pregnant. If you're going to have sex with someone you aren't in love with, you're going to get HIV. God forbid you have a one night stand with some hot stranger! Because then you'll find yourself lying in a gutter with your throat slit, have a raging case of herpes and pregnant with a rapists' child. It's called the "scare tactic", and our parents and school systems have used it on us for years when it comes to sex, drugs, alcohol or any other possible unsafe action, because they aren't certain if we are mature enough to know the truth. Well Kids, the truth is if you do these things safely, the chances are-you'll be fine. But there is **no guarantee**.

One in four Americans have an STI. *Ew.* That alone would make me want to use a condom. Now, out of those infected people, one in four of them are teens. Ok, I'm going to write it again. *Ew.* Just think… If you have had sexual encounters with four different partners (kissing, sex, fisting, etc.), you've probably been exposed to an STI. That doesn't necessarily mean that if you have had sex with four people you HAVE an STI. There's always a chance that you're an STI ninja and have had sex with an infected person several times but always came out clean. But just in case, you'd better get tested! Or, you can avoid the testing… And the treatment… And let one of the following fester up inside of your body. *Sounds tempting, doesn't it?!?*

There are at least twenty-five STIs, but I'm only going to touch base on the major ones:

HIV/AIDS

Human Immunodeficiency Virus (HIV)/Acquired Immune Deficiency Syndrome (AIDS) is the most well-known "STI" because of the scare in the 1980s. (I put "STI" in quotes because HIV/AIDS are not considered infections.) Even though it is the most feared, what people don't know is that it is not the most infectious STI and depending on the class and race of people you sexually frequent, it may not be one of the top STIs of your concern. Although, women beware! You are twice as likely to catch HIV, due to your thin, vaginal lining.

These aren't two different stages of one virus; they are actually two different viruses. HIV is considered a retrovirus, and is the primary viral agent for AIDS. What that means is that HIV doesn't necessarily turn into AIDS, but it causes AIDS. AIDS generally occurs when your CD4, or T cell count drops below 200. This usually takes at least ten years from when one first becomes infected with HIV.

HIV/AIDS can be transmitted by sex, drugs, biting (Vamps-beware!), and there have even traces of HIV found in the tears and sweat of AIDS patients! As for kissing, there is a report here and there, but I wouldn't worry about it. Just keep in mind; if you cut yourself while brushing your teeth, it takes up to a few hours for that to heal. So, if you plan on kissing someone, stick to gum or buy a soft-bristled toothbrush.

It's not curable, but due to the improvement of protease inhibitors (PIs), over the past few decades, the death drop from AIDS has decreased up to 70%-which is great! Most people infected with HIV/AIDS today can still live up to forty years. But get this-you need to be TREATED in order to live that long! One in every five people who have HIV in America don't even know that they have it! Thanks to the FDA though, home testing kits are now available! Do you know how exciting that is?!?! It's like Christmas! This will help the 8,000+ people who don't return to get the results of their STI testing each year. (Come on, don't be a pansy! You've gone this far!)

Hepatitis A, B, C, D, E, X & G

A is what you get when you visit Mexico. Just kidding. But you do get it from drinking infected water or food. You can also get this from oral and anal sex. Out of all of the Heps that affect your liver, this one is the least of your worries. Almost everyone survives it. And luckily, there is a vaccination available! But if worse comes to worse, after some excessive vomiting and explosive diarrhea, you'll be good as new.

B is spread through blood, semen, and other types of bodily fluids (such as vag juice). Don't share your friends' razors, and make sure your tattoo artist has enough money to pay for sterilized equipment. As for you injectable drug users, over 30% of you have this STI. As for you drug-free people who like sleeping with druggies, Hep B is 100 times more infectious than HIV. So run! Run far away from people with track marks. When people are infected with this Hep, their liver swells, and it can lead into a chronic illness. So, get your vaccination and be safe!

C is the worst of the seven. It has now stolen the title from HIV/AIDS and is considered the "deadliest" of all STIs, especially in jails. Unfortunately, there is no vaccination. In America, Hep C is four times more common than HIV. (Now how fucked up is that, considering it's not one of the standard tests offered during STI testing?) This 'silent killer', just like B affects the liver. For all of you alcoholics out there, you're screwed if you get any of these. It's like a double whammy for your liver; and cirrhosis, hardening of the liver, will prevail. It's spread like all of the other STIs, so once again, stop your vampire role-playing and use condoms.

D, again, is another liver disease. But here's the good news! You can't get D, unless you have B! So, get your vaccination for B and you'll be good to go!

E is another Mexican disease. Again, I kid! It's just like A... Not as serious as the others.

Ever notice that when scientists don't know what something is, they refer to it as "**X**", i.e. Planet X. Well, this "unknown" Hep has been labeled as "X" because it doesn't fall into any of the other categories.

G was discovered around the same time as C, but they know less about it because less people have been infected, and it is asymptomatic. So, stick to your safety rules and hope your Hep G free!

HPV

The Human Papilloma Virus is the most prevalent in sexually active people today. More than 80% of sexually active people get this STI in their lifetime, and as of now there is no cure. The reason why so many people get this is because until recently, only women were able to get tested. Therefore, men were rampantly spreading the virus around unknowingly. Now, they're still rarely getting testing because the test involves a swab in the urethra; and he'd have to be a severe masochist to want to undergo a feeling similar to an ice pick being hammered into his dick.

Also, it's really easy to catch HPV. Other than the obvious ways one can catch an STI, you can actually catch it from skin-to-skin contact. So, you can dry hump all you want and you won't get pregnant, but there's a good chance you'll get HPV if your partner's infected.

There are over 100 strains of HPV. Some cause penile/cervical cancer and some cause warts. Depending on what type you have, you may have to deal with it the rest of your life or it may disappear on its own. Just to be safe and get the vaccination!

Herpes

The Herp. In my opinion, this one is the most annoying, because it's not going to kill you, but it's still nasty to have. And unlike a nasty period, it comes and goes as it pleases. You can't plan out the times you're going to have a breakout.

There are twenty-five strains of the Herpes Simplex Virus (HSV), including HSV1, HSV2, chicken pox, shingles and mono. So yes, if you've had chicken pox as a child, you technically have had herpes; but, the STI forms that everyone fears are HSV1 and HSV2.

Now it is commonly thought that HSV1 is in the mouth and HSV2 is in the genital region. This is not necessarily true. You can get either one in either place. For instance, if your significant other has a cold sore in their mouth, goes down on you and their braces cut you, you could get HSV1 on your dick. And if your partner has HSV2 in her pussy and you just finished brushing your teeth with a hard-bristled toothbrush, you could get HSV2 in your mouth. What's even more fucking nasty is that you can get either of these anywhere on your body! So, if your girlfriend chews her fingernails and you suck on her fingers, she could get herpes blisters all over her fingers! *Now that's hot!* Better buy some of those finger condoms! (And yes… I'm serious… They do exist.)

No, there is no cure for this impractical disease, but they do have treatments and topical creams. Ending on a positive note, "topical" sounds like "tropical", so go make yourself a margarita.

Chlamydia

Chlamydia, Gonorrhea, and Syphilis all go together. You can be infected with more than one at a time, so when you have one, you are tested for the other two. But it really doesn't matter if you have one, two or all three, because finally, we've come across some STIs that CAN be cured!

Chlamydia is a bacterial infection that is extremely common in sexually active people. Undiagnosed Chlamydia can lead to further damage in a woman's cervix, and a man's urethra. This infection is responsible for 20% of infertile women, so it is important if you are sexually active for you to get tested for this on a regular basis.

Gonorrhea

Gonorrhea is also caused by bacteria that grow in moist areas. The bacteria can even be found growing in people's eyes; so when you're going down on your partner, use a condom to protect your mouth and perhaps some protective eyewear in case of any squirting.

Like box jellies, we don't have to worry about it yet; but, there is a 'Super' Gonorrhea that has been discovered in Japan in 2008. Supposedly it is resistant to every medicine scientists are testing on it. Hopefully, it will be stopped before it makes its way on this side of the globe.

Syphilis
This is the oldest of the bunch, and had once spread like wild flowers amongst the artists from the Renaissance Era. Luckily today, it is not as serious as it used to be, and most of our modern musicians are not infected with this STI. I guess they found another way to get their creative juices flowing! Hopefully, we'll be saying that about the ones listed above sooner than later. Again, it's another bacterial infection, so it's curable; but, if left untreated, it can lead to paralysis, brain or heart damage, and even death. Be careful if you ever come down with Syphilis sores, because it increases the chances of you acquiring HIV by ~5%. Again, get tested on a regular basis and thank Sir Alexander Flemming for not keeping a clean lab.

Crabs
Is that a beach in your pants, or do you just have crabs? Crabs... The funniest of all the STIs. Why are they called crabs? Because the mature stage of the organism looks like a crab! No, they do not walk sideways. And no, shaving your pubes is not the answer; although, your partner may suggest it for aesthetic purposes.

Crabs are technically pubic lice; but, they are also found in other areas like leg hair, armpits, and mustaches. Now that's fucking funny! What's not so funny is that if pubic lice are found on the eyelashes of a child, it could be an indication of child molestation. Generally, the lice on your head are "head lice", but if your partner likes getting all up in their while they're giving you "head", there's a chance that a little nymph will jump from your groin to their head of hair. *Whoops!* Luckily, if you have a dog or cat that likes curling up in your pelvic area while you're sleeping they don't have to worry about catching your crabs. Only humans can get and spread pubic lice.

Trichomoniasis

Trichomoniasis is caused by a parasite, like crabs. It is spread through genital contact, but luckily this parasite cannot live in the mouth or anus. *Yay!*

This STI can be treated with an antibiotic; but once again, if left untreated, it can do damage to areas like the cervix. So, remember to specify for this one too when you're ordering your tests.

As you may have noticed in the above section, I did not discuss any symptoms of the listed STIs. I did this purposely. This isn't fucking *WebMD*. **I didn't write this chapter to try to give you a complex and make you think you have some deadly disease. I'm writing this to help you become more educated and accepting of sexuality; and in turn, expect you to make healthy decisions. Depending on the STI and the time of infection, over 90% of people are asymptomatic. What this means is that they express no warning signs that their bodies are under attack. Here is TayloR Puck's warning sign:** <u>**If you are sexually active, you are exposing your body to STIs. SO GET TESTED!**</u>

For those of you who choose to "plead ignorance", and aren't mature enough to handle the consequences (even though you *think* you're mature enough to participate in sexual acts), conjure up the courage to get tested just once! Get your close friends involved too. Make it a group activity! This is a great sorority/fraternity activity. It promotes the sisterly and brotherly relationships and healthy choices. Getting tested for STIs on a regular basis is one of the most healthy, routine habits. I'm not saying the first time is easy! But if you do it on a regular basis, you'll instinctively make better decisions when it comes to sexual activities. Not only will your partners have respect for you, but you will too.

Speaking of partners: If you're one who has a large number of people you've had sex with and dread having the person you're interested in ask you what your "number" is; if you've been tested recently it douses the question a bit. What I mean by that is, if a naïve, sweet girl is on a date with a manwhore and asks him how many girls he's slept with… If his answer is, "That I remember?" she very well may excuse herself to the Ladies' Room and never return. Whereas, if his answer is more along the lines of, "I've had my fair share… But I get tested on a regular basis and I always make sure I'm playing it safe," her plans on how far she intends on going with him that night will not fade into thin air. She'll accept that his number is high, and respect his decision to stay safe.

For those of you who are diagnosed with an incurable STI, life is far from over. The thoughts, "No one will ever date me again!" or "What will <fill in the blank> think?!" will inevitably cross your mind. But like every shocking experience, time will help the healing process and you will learn to live life with the added factor. This is why it's important to test yourself now, so you can start treatment as soon as possible. Always make your health top priority.

Yes, some STIs have no cure, but they aren't considered "terminal" like they used to be. With medications and proper condom usage, an infected person can still remain in an intimate relationship with someone who is STI-free! That is, as long as the partner can mentally grasp the fact that there are ways to reduce the transmission-factor to almost zero percent. And with a little counseling here and there, they should be convinced. If not, there's www.PositiveSingles.com! Amazing! Is there anything online dating CAN'T do?!

REFERENCES:

Caufield, P. (2012). 'Super' gonorrhea sweeping the globe, health experts warn. *NY Daily News.* Retrieved from http://articles.nydailynews.com/2012-06-06/news/32084585_1_gonorrhea-antibiotic-resistant-strain-std

Centers for Disease Control and Prevention. (2010). *Syphilis-CDC fact sheet.* Retrieved from http://www.cdc.gov/std/syphilis/stdfact-syphilis.htm

Cichocki, M. (2007). *What is a CD4 count and why is it important?* Retrieved from http://aids.about.com/od/technicalquestions/f/cd4.htm HIV and AIDS. (2012). Retrieved from http://www.centrahealth.com/health-library/h/399-hiv-and-aids

Jones, R. & Lopez, K. *Human Reproductive Biology. (3rd Ed.).* Amsterdam: Academic Press.

Medical News Today. (2009). *What is hepatitis? Symptoms, causes and treatments.* Retrieved from http://www.medicalnewstoday.com/articles/145869.php

MedicineNet.com. (2010) *Pubic Lice (Crabs).* Retrieved from http://www.medicinenet.com/pubic_lice_crabs/article.htm

Medscape Education. (2012). *Importance and practicalities of patient's counseling in the prevention and management of genital herpes.* Retrieved from http://www.medscape.org/viewarticle/48996

Prison's deadliest inmate, hepatitis C, escaping. (2007, March 14). *MBC News.* Retrieved from http://www.msnbc.msn.com/id/17615346/ns/health-infectious_diseases/t/prisons-deadliest-inmate-hepatitis-c-escaping/

Public Health Agency of Canada. (2004). *Hepatitis G Fact Sheet.* Retrieved from http://www.phac-aspc.gc.ca/hcai-iamss/bbp-pts/hepatitis/hep_g-eng.php

PubMed Health. (2010). *Chlamydia.* Retrieved from http://www.ncbi.nlm.nih.gov/pubmedhealth/PMH0002321/

PubMed Health. (2011). *Gonorrhea.* Retrieved from http://www.ncbi.nlm.nih.gov/pubmedhealth/PMH0004526/

Ranker, L. (2012). *New HIV test to be available this fall.* Retrieved from http://www.republic-online.com/news/article_7ca84fbb-405d-52ea-9a89-12a6ab567d5d.html

SafeLab Centre. (2012). *STD statistics and information about STD testing.* Retrieved from http://www.safelabcentre.com/std-statistics.html

San Francisco AIDS Foundation. (2012). *HIV basics.* Retrieved from http://www.sfaf.org/hiv-info/basics/

Southern Nevada Health District. (2012). *Syphilis.* Retrieved from http://www.southernnevadahealthdistrict.org/syphilis/quickfacts.php

Stibich, M. (2009). *HIV/AIDS drugs increase life expectancy.* Retrieved from http://longevity.about.com/od/longevityandillness/a/HIV-AIDS-life.htm

TeenHealthFX. (2009). *Difference between STD and STI.* Retrieved from http://teenhealthfx.com/answers/sexuality+sexual+health/44602

Vachani, C. (n.d.). Over 100 strains of HPV-Nocure. Retrieved from http://rense.com/general75/100.htm

Van Vranken, M. (2007). Prevention and treatment of sexually transmitted diseases: An update. *American Family Physician.* 76(12).

This circle of sexuality revolves around how we perceive ourselves as a sexual being. Its major components consist of: Biological sex, sexual orientation, gender identity, and gender role.

BOYS HAVE A PENIS,
GIRLS HAVE A VULVA

"**I**s it a boy or girl?" This is the first question popped when the message has been relayed that we even exist. People want to know: Will they be buying you blue or pink gifts? Funny how the first question is never: "Is the baby healthy?" —*shows where our cultural priorities lie.* The parents' first reactions usually revolve around the healthiness of the child; for some, the sex of the baby is irrelevant. But for those parents who keep the sex of their babies a surprise, it *truly* is a surprise if the doctor looks up from behind the sheets after hearing the notorious inquiry, "Is it a boy or a girl?" and answers back, "Flip a coin…"

From the little sex education that you did receive from your schooling, you should know that the biological sex of a person describes their genetic make-up, hormones, and sexual and reproductive anatomy. Put simply: The biological sex describes whether someone is a boy or girl. What determines the sex? Well chromosomally, your father does; gonadally, whether or not you have ovaries or testicles; and hormonally, your levels of estrogen and androgen. As astonishing as it may seem, sometimes these three biological factors aren't always so clear-cut!

The sex of a child can usually be determined around 18-20 weeks in utero. "Why so late?" you may ask. The early stages of development are determined by the mother's genotype. This is because it takes about three weeks for the embryo's DNA to kick in and start molding the actual embryo. At eight weeks, the embryo is large enough to be labeled a fetus; and the organs begin to develop. "Indifferent gonads" begin to take shape but do not grow into ovaries or testes until they receive further instructions. If the baby has a Y chromosome, it carries the SRY gene; this gene promotes the protein, H-Y antigen. And it is this protein which activates the process of turning the fetus into a male.

Both male and female babies have two systems when they are born: the Wolffian system and the Mullerian system. IF the baby has a Y chromosome, the attached SRY gene allows for the secretion of the H-Y antigen. Then, the H-Y antigen will bring about change in the gonads by turning them into testes. In reaction to the production of the testes, testosterone materializes and the Wolffian system develops into the vas deferens and the seminal vesicles. As a result, the Mullerian system, which is not in use, will disintegrate. Conversely, if the fetus does not receive spurts of testosterone, the Wolffian system will not develop, which will catalyze the production of the Mullerian system. The final result: a uterus, fallopian tubes and a vagina will appear. To simplify: Development of the Wolffian system=blue presents; Development of the Mullerian system=pink presents.

For most of you, the Wolffian and Mullerian systems are new vocabulary terms; you've simply been taught that when you are born, you're either a boy (with XY chromosomes), or a girl (with double X chromosomes). It's understandable that you haven't been taught about other chromosomal options. I mean, how many times have you had a heart to heart talk with your parents regarding your chromosomal mixture? Probably never. But chromosomal abnormalities aren't so "abnormal" after all!

Different chromosomal combinations occur regularly in our world. Any abnormality can occur during the development of an egg or sperm. How? Who the fuck knows? But one thing's for sure: any person that is born with abnormal chromosomes was born for a reason; and that, my Friends, is something to really think about. The truth is that more than half of the miscarriages that occur take place because of chromosomal abnormality (and the majority of miscarriages are male). So, if you know someone who has defied science in the womb, they deserve your awe and respect, at the very least.

The majority of people have 46 chromosomes. The first 22 pairs are called autosomes; and the last pair are the sex chromosomes. Chromosomal abnormalities can occur on autosomes or sex chromosomes. Probably the most well-known autosomal abnormality is Down syndrome. This affects about 1 in 800 babies, and is a result from a third copy of chromosome 21. Although the outlook for Down syndrome children is far greater than it once was, the risk of this trisomy occurring, as well as others, is present and greatly increases with the mother's age. Two other trisomies that occur less commonly are Trisomy 13 (Patau syndrome) and Trisomy 18 (Edwards syndrome). One of the reasons why these two are not more ingrained in your brain is because you probably don't know anyone who has either of these abnormalities. Sadly, babies born with Trisomies 13 or 18 do not usually live beyond their first birthday.

Sex chromosomal abnormalities are usually less talked about because for the most part, they are less noticeable. Turner syndrome (XO), which affects about 1 in 2,500 girls is when a girl has one full X chromosome, but is missing parts of or all of her second X chromosome. Girls who are affected with this syndrome are usually born with webbing between their fingers and toes, short, infertile and do not undergo normal puberty changes; unless treated with hormone treatments. The male equivalent to this syndrome is the Noonen syndrome. It can cause a small penis, undescended testicles, delayed puberty, sunken in chests and slanted eyes and ears in males; although, it can affect females as well too. People with this syndrome usually have trouble with relationships. Even more frequent in males, is the Klinefelter syndrome. Boys born with this syndrome have two or more X chromosomes accompanying their single Y chromosome. Boys affected with this abnormality are usually very tall, with long arms and legs, and are infertile. Other variants of this syndrome include karyotypes such as XXYY and XXXYY.

Less drastic chromosomal abnormalities are Triple X, which affects girls; and XYY, which affects boys. Both of these abnormalities may result in learning difficulties; but unless tested, the majority of the time people have these genetic anomalies, they aren't even aware of it! Another one that occurs in males is XYY. Excessive aggression is known to occur in these males, and a stereotype that is associated with this abnormality is that the majority of them end up in jail! As crazy as it may seem, there are even more complicated chromosomal abnormalities that science is just beginning to discover. One can also have structural abnormalities, which involve deletions, microdeletions, translocations, inversions, duplications, or ring chromosomes.

Any person who is born with sex chromosomes that simply aren't XY or XX are known to be intersex. But as mentioned from above, unless tested for sex chromosomal abnormalities, intersex isn't always obvious. In some cases, a person born as an intersex is much more noticeable. This is when the child is born with ambiguous genitalia.

Ambiguous genitalia refer to genitals that aren't clearly defined as a male's or female's. For instance, a female may have an oversized clitoris, or lack a vaginal opening; whereas, a male may be born with a not so well-endowed penis, or divided scrotum (resembling more of a vulva; rather than a sac). It is important to know that the correct terminology to use is the term "intersex"; not "hermaphrodite". Hermaphrodites are living creatures with both full-blown, fully-functional male and female reproductive organs. We are not frogs, snails nor plants; human beings are not born with both. So, no matter what Jamie Lee Curtis' crotch contained when she was born, the rumor that she is a hermaphrodite is a lie.

If you have not already taken a moment between the last paragraph and this one and to *Google* images of ambiguous genitalia, take a moment and satisfy your itch…

Now that I have your focus back, I would like to shock you with the fact that more than 1 out of every 2,000 babies are born with an intersex condition. How many people are in your high school? If the number is over 2,000, you probably know a couple of people born with one of these phenomenons!

So, we've already discussed that the chromosomal abnormalities are sometimes unknown when a child is born. But when a child is born with ambiguous genitalia, it's a different story. A decision is made by the parents, after being informed by the doctor; although, it has been said that sometimes the doctors do more than simply inform. Politically speaking, the doctors should "provide", not "suggest" options. Either way, a decision is eventually made by the parents, and either surgery is performed on the child's genitals or the child is raised to a mature age and given the choice to manipulate their own genitalia.

Parents dream of being able to pick the sex of their baby. And much research, not necessarily valid, has been conducted to find out how to manipulate the chosen sperm. For instance, according to studies, factors that have been known to alter the sex ratio are as follows: diet, vaginal pH, father's profession, time of year, annual rainfall, time of menstrual cycle and birth rank. According to Dr. Landrum Shettles, certain positions are suggested for boy-desiring parents or girl-desiring parents. It is well known that male sperm (carrying the Y-chromosome) are smaller, faster, and shorter-lived. For parents who crave a boy, it's better for them to have sex at the exact time of ovulation. This way, the little Speedy Gonzalez will win the race and meet the egg in the fallopian tube. On the other hand, parents who desire a little girl are told to have sex in the missionary position two to four days before ovulation. This is because the female sperm last longer and will patiently swim around and watch the Y's die off. When the egg finally appears, they'll be the only ones left with the chance of conquering the fertilization.

Parents will research ALL of this shit JUST before fucking, because some parents will try ANYTHING to specifically aim for a boy or a girl. So, it may seem that if a parent had a choice when the day of their child's birth finally arrived to choose the sex of their baby, it would be a positive thing! But I can assure you; under no circumstances is this a choice a parent wants to come upon. Picture this:

A woman is eagerly giving birth to her third child. Her husband is holding her hand and delightfully encouraging her to push. They have kept the sex of the baby a secret. They hear a cry. The baby is cleaned and a cheerful statement from the nurse gives indication that the baby is healthy. But the smiling husband and wife are becoming impatient and confused as to why the sex of the baby has not been revealed yet. The doctor walks over and slightly huddles with the medical team. The parents' smiling faces fade into looks of concern.

The doctors, i.e. endocrinologist, genealogist, gynecologist and so on, inform the parents that the child has been born with ambiguous genitalia. They are going to perform a series of tests, and then the parents will have some decisions to make. The test results will provide the chromosomal analysis by recognizing any other birth defects, as well as skeletal abnormalities. These results will be available within a few days.

"A few days!?!" the father cries. "What do we tell our friends when they ask if 'it's' a boy or girl?!"

"We suggest that you tell your family members and friends that the sex has not been determined yet," a doctor replies. "We know this is a stressful situation, but we do have counselors at the hospital to help you through this."

The medical team leaves the couple alone. They inform a nurse to tell the people in the waiting room that there are medical problems with the baby, and they don't know if the baby is going to make it. Please respect their privacy, and they will be in touch.

The couple begins to discuss their trepidations. Ultimately, they know that surgery can be done to change their baby's genitals to make them look "normal". But what if the chromosomal analysis doesn't reveal an exact sex? Should they be the ones to make the decision on what sex the child should be? If so, what if they choose the wrong sex? It could psychologically destroy him/her! What if the child ends up experiencing a gender-identiy crisis? What if they let the child grow up with the ambiguous genitalia and let them decide what to do when they are older? How old do they have to be? At what age is a child old enough to firmly make the decision on what sex they want to be? And won't that psychologically destroy him/her as well? How is it going to affect the family? What do they tell the other family members? And the child's siblings!?! How do they raise the child?

"This is God's job, NOT OURS!" the father yells as he falls to his knees and begins to bawl.

You may be questioning your genitalia and chromosomal combination after reading the above information. And if so? Good! But, if you'd like to know more, I'd suggest NOT bringing it up at the dinner table. It may result in everyone losing their appetites; which would waste the dinner that your mom, dad or the Chinese people around the corner slaved over for the past hour. Keep in mind, don't ask anything if you're not mature and understanding enough to know the answer. Chances are, like being dealt a pair of aces in poker, you're safe. But if your parents do divulge some disturbing details, remember that they love you and are your support group. The only things they want for you are health, happiness and success. And if they were put in a position to make a decision on your behalf, or have kept a decision that they have made from you, it's only because they love you. When is it the correct time to tell your child, "By the way…"? After their first piano recital? Perhaps, one afternoon when they come home from the mall? I'm telling you, if your parents have been put in a decision where they had to make a choice regarding your genitals, like a person who's hiding out in the closet, it is something they've been struggling with every moment of your life. So, if you choose to open up the bag of gummy worms and ask the questions; do not freak out, do not judge, and do not blame. Communicate. Because your understanding and communication can possibly relieve the stress of a lifetime.

P.S. If you're going to see if there's a cat in the bag, and ask your parents such sensitive questions regarding your birth, you might as well throw in the question of whether or not your mom pooped while giving birth to you-for shits and giggles (pun intended). Chances on that one are somewhat higher than you being born intersex, considering 39% of women defecate while giving birth.

REFERENCES:

American Pregnancy Association. (2012). Ultrasound: Sonogram. Retrieved from http://www.americanpregnancy.org/prenataltesting/ultrasound.html

Anonymous. (2012, July 10). Interview by TayloR Puck. Ambiguous Genitalia. Kaiser Permanente Hospital, San Francisco, CA.

Baby Center. (2012). Your pregnancy: 30 weeks. Retrieved from http://www.babycenter.com/6_your-pregnancy-30-weeks_1119.bc

Crane, B. (2008, September 20). *Male/Female*. Human Sexuality Program, Widener University, Chester, Pennsylvania.

Ericsson RJ. (1976). [X and Y spermatozoa]. *Contraception, Fertilite, Sexualite*. 4(8), 655-68.

Intersex Society of North America. (2008). Is a person who is intersex a hermaphrodite? Retrieved from http://www.isna.org/faq/hermaphrodite

March of Dimes. (2009). Birth defects. Retrieved from http://www.marchofdimes.com/baby/birthdefects_chromosomal.html/

Shettles, L.B. & Rorvik, D.M. (1997). *How To Choose the Sex of Your Baby*. New York: Broadway Books.

University of Texas. (n.d.) Review of Sexual Differentiation. Retrieved from http://homepage.psy.utexas.edu/homepage/class/psy308/humm/reviewofsexualdifferentiation

WHAT'S IN YOUR CLOSET?

N ow when I hear the term, "in the closet", the first thing I wonder is, "What type of closet is it? Is it a walk-in closet? Are there French doors? Perhaps there is a 7½ pair of pink *Louboutins* that are located inside, just *waiting* to be worn… Or maybe a sweet-ass *Dolce* Dress!" *Mmmm…. It puts a smile on my face just thinking about it.* But in all seriousness, no wonder gay people hide out in these little cubbies because they're too afraid to let the cat out of the bag! Closets are comfy! And safe, for that matter! Think about it… If there's a tornado and someone's already in the tub, "Shotgun the closet, Bitches!"

The whole idea of "coming out" started with Gay activist, Karl Heinrich Ulrichs in the late 19th Century. Ulrichs created the homosexuality term, "Uranismus", which was in reference to Venus Urania, the Greek Goddess of the "Gays". (Bet you didn't learn about this one in Greek Mythology!) This German homosexual rights advocate urged other fellow gays to be proud of their orientation and take the risk to come out to society. This was definitely known as a risk, considering that back then, gays were thought to be mentally ill. This didn't change until 1973, due to the hard work of Dr. Evelyn Hooker (ha ha), and other psychological professionals, who were able to remove homosexuality from the Diagnostic and Statistical Manual of Mental Disorders (DSM). So the answer to the notorious question, "Who was treated like equals first: the blacks or the gays?" is the blacks. This sure makes white heterosexuals look like assholes, doesn't it?

The whole closet appendage evolved from the idiom, "skeleton in the closet". It stemmed from the idea that one has a secret that they are storing in their closet. I really don't care for this idea, considering I dream of large, spacious closets with expensive apparel and accessories. I'd prefer that there would be no rotting, or decaying bodies accompanying me in *my* closet. But then again, I suppose if one were struggling with their sexual identity every waking second (~57,600 waking seconds/day), that would be quite stressful... Especially if they're claustrophobic.

So, how gay are you? (If your head voice is answering in a disgusted tone right now, "What the fuck!?! I'm not fucking gay!" think again, little ignant child.) It just so turns out, we're all a little gay! But let's word ourselves correctly here. If you're only *partially* gay, that would mean you're bisexual. So next time someone asks you what your sexual orientation is, you'd be lying through your teeth if you didn't answer, "Bisexual". Don't believe me? Well, let's look at the research, shall we?

Doctor Alfred Kinsey is the man! Born in New Jersey... Figures... He was one of the first scientists to dive into the Human Sexuality field. He is well-known for the his research institute, The Kinsey Institute for Research in Sex, Gender, and Reproduction, his theories on human sexual behavior, and the notorious Kinsey Scale. The Kinsey Scale is a sexual orientation rating scale, ranging from zero to six. Zero represents exclusive heterosexuality and six represents exclusive homosexuality. For those of you who have never heard of this scale, it's not a test with a right or wrong answer. It's more like a personal reflection, where *you* decide where you fall on the continuum. Just be honest with yourself, and see what happens. What's even more interesting is that your view on where you lie on the Kinsey Scale changes during each period of your life. So, if at the moment, you think you are strictly a zero, three, or six, that's fine. You're young, and you have many

Sexual Identity

experiences awaiting you. Just remember to evaluate yourself again every five years. You'll be shocked to see how your view of your own sexuality changes, once you've experienced some fun, crazy shit! But give me a moment… I want to have some fun with you so-called "zero"s…

If you're a female, and you rate yourself as a zero on the Kinsey Scale, picture this: You're walking down the streets of New York City, and you're passing hundreds of people per minute. You look up to see two random people walking in your direction. One is a gorgeous, built man in his twenties and the other is a sexy, fit woman in her twenties. Which one do you think you focus on first? The answer is the woman. Why? Because women are hot! And probably because you're a bit self-conscious of your own body and are searching relentlessly to find some flaw in her so you can feel better about yourself. Plain and simple: research shows that over fifty percent of heterosexual women admit they are sexually attracted to other women, and over fifty percent have also had sexual experiences with other women. I know 50% doesn't seem like a crazy lot, but just think-these are the only women who *admit* it!

If you're a guy right now who rates themselves a zero on the Kinsey Scale, you're probably getting a woody from the above paragraph. But let's focus on you for a moment. I'd like to help you maintain your woody and bring your attention to porn. Imagine your favorite heterosexual flick. It probably involves a woman getting fucked by a guy. Possibly multiple guys! Maybe you're envisioning a blow bang, where a female is on her knees, performing fellatio to the ring of men surrounding her. Slutty… And hot! But let me ask you this: If you're a 100% straight male, why the hell are you jacking off to other naked dudes? You may argue that you are focusing on the female and the actions she's performing… But, hello!?!? You can't deny that there are other cocks in your view! Now, if you were *truly* heterosexual, and the thought of another man made you soft, you probably wouldn't be able to enjoy porn now, would you? (Sorry if your woody is now fading...)

Still think you're a zero? Go rent the movie *Shortbus*, then. And when you're done watching that, rerate yourself on Kinsey's scale. Whether you're "straight", "gay", "bi", or even "asexual" (and yes, people do identify as this sexual orientation, or lack thereof) -this movie will awaken sexual attractions that you never knew you even had. And once your sexual senses are stimulated, you'll understand Kinsey's sex continuum even more! For all of you non-believers out there who think there are only straight people and gay people (it's called monosexism) you're wrong. Take your Neapolitan ice cream for example... If you like vanilla, strawberry and chocolate ice cream, is it because you're confused? Hell no! It's because you like them all! Sometimes you want vanilla, sometimes you want strawberry, sometimes you want chocolate, and sometimes (when you're *really* in the ice cream orgy mode) you want a scoop of all three! Being bisexual **does not** mean you're confused. Are there people your age who are confused regarding their orientation? Hell yeah! There are people in their *fifties* who are confused about their orientation! But I assure you: There are other orientations, other than the two ends of Kinsey's dichotomy.

While you're in the midst of scrutinizing your own sexual orientation for the moment, wondering if you drunkingly making out with Sara at Ryan's party last weekend means you like a little strawberry, or just means you're a drunkin' slut, let me bring up the age-old, homosexuality question, here: Nature vs. nurture? Was your slutty episode a choice, because you wanted Ryan's attention? Or did you submissively let her stick her tongue down your throat because the slutty, red-headed bitch *actually* sexually aroused you? You can argue that homosexuality is innate or a choice all you want. In fact, biologists and social theorists (or how I like to refer to them: Scientists and Church folks) do all of the time! But even though there has been evidence revealing that a gay man's hypothalamus is structurally different than a straight man's, or that high doses of androgen in the prenatal stage may lead to homosexuality, there is still no significant data proving sociologists, like Foucault and Halperin, wrong. These men believe that homosexuality is simply an error, or preference. My favorite argument which is always asserted by the most *scientific intellectuals*: "Because the bible says..."

"Fuck it!" That's what I like to say. The truth is, there are both men and women who claim they choose homosexuality/bisexuality; but, there are even more men and women who claim that their sexual orientation is *not* a choice. Whether or not people want it to exist, it does. Homosexual orientation affects about ten percent of our population and is constant across cultures. So until we come up with valid research proving one over the other, we're just going to have to believe everyone and accept everyone's sexual orientation-no matter what color it is, and have fun!

We may not be able to determine whether the cause of non-heterosexuality is due to nature or nurture, but what we can determine is that it is "natural". It's ok! Being straight is natural! Being bisexual is natural! Being gay is natural! It just doesn't seem that way, because we grow up in a society where we we're raised to think that heterosexuality is the only natural way. Well, guess what?!?! It's NOT! Hetero<u>normality</u> has been socially constructed by us; our culture has sculpted heterosexuality to be the "norm". And the term "normal" is used to describe the average, or customary. So in turn, as more sexual orientations become more prevalent (which will continue to happen because our society is *slowly* becoming more tolerable of non-heteros), sexual orientations other than zeros will eventually be viewed as normal.

Still having a hard time trying to comprehend a non-hetero act as being natural? Let me try to simplify: Humans, like other animals, are sexual beings and we are attracted to certain things about each other. So no matter what gender the other person is, you're going to find something sexually appealing about them.

If that instigates some experimentation-bring it! As of now, we know of at least 1,500 species on Earth that experiment with homosexuality. Even the most masculine animal on the planet has been known to play a little penis popper in the pooper. That's right, Kids! Even Simba likes taking it up the ass! There is no shame! The only reason why we've been raised to think otherwise is because America is a little behind in the times when it comes to sexuality. I mean, come on! Homosexuality just got off the DSM less than forty years ago?!?! No wonder the gays have such an amazing fashion sense! If I spent half my life in a closet, I'd probably be able to come up with the most trendy styles too!

Half your life in a closet… What a scary thought. If you are an adolescent and have never experienced a secret about yourself that you've stowed so deeply into the back of your wardrobe, you'd better thank your lucky stars. Because even though it's been forty years, and the world is an easier place for gays to be themselves than it was ten years ago, and ten years before that, it's not that easy of a place. No matter what decade we are in, it's still a personal, social, and political challenge that creates an unnecessary, emotional rollercoaster for someone who finds themselves primarily attracted to the same sex. And why do they find peace and serenity in a small room filled with inanimate objects and no windows? Because of people. Possibly people like you. People who find comfort in judging homosexuals so that they can feel more like a zero, instead of a two. Think of the harsh, hetero-normative world that we live in today. This world has been created by zeros, with very little tolerance for ones through sixes. Is that fair? Imagine this:

You're a little alien, growing up on a planet where everyone's goal was to eat the most perfect roast beef sandwich. The culture revolved around the beef. The beef was farmed on a nearby prestigious planet, where only royalty lived. Since the roast beef sandwiches were in high demand, considering they were not native to the planet, young aliens had to wait to prove themselves in order for them to one day taste the juicy goodness. So, you worked your entire adolescence, dreaming of your first taste, and awaiting the best experience of your life.

Your parents wanted nothing more for you than for you to grow up and experience that sensational moment where the roast beef touched your lips. "He's such a great, little alien," they'd say. "We can't wait to see his little face when the day comes where he tries his first roast beef sandwich." Other little aliens would tease each other during their alien games. "My roast beef's going to be smellier than yours!" they'd yell at each other.

Then, the day came! (Now remember, you've spent your entire life waiting for this moment!) The curtains pulled away and there lay a brownish/pinkish, juicy roast beef sandwich. You took a bite, expecting ecstasy. But, your reaction was not what you expected it to be. *I do not like munching on this roast beef,* you thought. *I do not like it at all! Salami sandwiches are much better! Salami sandwiches make my mouth MUCH wetter!* Shit… You just came to the realization that you prefer salami over roast beef. Now what, Bitch?

Perhaps this Dr. Seussish/Rudolph the Red-Nosed Reindeer story sounded quite childish to you. But if after reading this chapter you're still intolerable to sexual orientations other than your own, you're the one with the issues. Can you say "homophobe"?

Over 90% of gay people have been verbally abused because of their sexuality. Now, as we all know, *every* teen gets verbally abused, bullied, or teased. Whatever you want to call it-it's safe to say that it is extremely difficult to survive these adolescent years. So on top of the regular teasing you receive from kids because you flail your arms around too much when you run, or because you have a mole on your face that makes you look like Enrique, add in another one hundred hours of bullying because of your sexual orientation. *One hundred hours!?!* I'm ball-parking it here-could be more, could be less... But I assure you, the aftermath of the bullying received by a non-hetero teen is much more devastating than the average teen. Could you deal with one hundred hours of bullying? Of course! You'd live! And if you took all of the bullying in one shot, that would only be ~4 days! But if you were ridiculed for four days straight because of something that you had no control over; something that made you *YOU*—how would you deal with the remnants of your self-confidence? Would you be able to pick up the pieces and move on? Possibly. But the memories of those four days would never go away. Now in reality, those four days of bullying are not confined to four consecutive days, but spread out over the most tumultuous years of one's life. People who have non-hetero tendencies deal with negative words, stares—rejections of all kinds, all day long, all of the time. It's bad enough that they're going through their own personal identity crisis! They have to deal with self doubt regarding their faith, parents and sense of selves. Now add in the peer bullying!?!? Hit them while they're down, why don't ya?

As a zero, you probably have no clue to how this would feel, considering it's very unusual for a straight boy to be ridiculed for eating too much pussy, or a straight girl to be teased because she prefers the salami over the beef. But let's discuss a homosexual's worst enemy. George Weinberg labeled these gay haters as "homophobes", which describes someone that has an *irrational* fear, hatred or intolerance of homosexuals. Notice how I italicized the word "irrational". Now, I'd like to ask you to take a moment and put some rational thought towards such an irrational behavior. Ok, everyone has a right to have their own opinion; but why, exactly, would one hate someone else based on their sexual orientation? Why would you even give a shit to who they're attracted to? Let's psychoanalyze, shall we?

Going back to Freud's Oedipus complex, some scientists associate homophobia to latent homosexuality. Remember back to your science class-latent means stored. So, these psychologists are assuming that people who suffer from homophobia have stored homosexual thoughts that they are either consciously unaware of, or are simply in denial. Either way, they believe that the angry and uncomfortable outbursts of homophobic acts are just a product of their inner gayness trying to escape. Unfortunately, the relationship between latent homosexuality and homophobia has not been extensively investigated. The one empirical study that determined that men who suffer from homophobia do get sexually aroused from seeing homosexual activities-proves nothing! We already established the fact that we're all a little bi! So, we're just going to throw this theory out the window, or at least put it aside on the sill for the time being.

The truth is, whether homophobia is a result from inflexible morals, sexual ignorance, or fear of non-hetero acts, the answer to the question, "Where does homophobia stem from?" is unknown. I, like other professionals, like to theorize it as a social construct, rather than a psychological phobia. And who do I ultimately blame for homophobia? Parents. Think about it. How does a child become a hick? Because their redneck parents raised them to be that way! The same thing goes for *Nascar* fans, and same thing goes for the *WWE* fans. Why do these kids think these things are cool? It's probably because their uneducated, ignorant parents steered them in that direction. I mean, I know there are exceptions…. But I'm just sayin'…

So remember, no matter what your influences are or have been, or what you've learned or have not learned about sexual orientation, you're going to get mixed messages. This is why you need to keep an open mind and not judge people on their sexual orientation. It's easy to stereotype gay men as being skinny with high-pitched voices, who party a lot and live in Greenwich Village. Hell! I used to work in the Village! And yes! These men *do* exist! But what about bears? And no, I do not mean Grizzlies or Polars. A bear is a slang term that describes an overweight, hairy man in the gay community. Try meeting one of them with a deep voice and then argue that you have impeccable "gaydar". The same goes for lipstick lesbians! These feminine lezzies exhibit their sexy swagger and are more made up than a celebrity walking down the red carpet (aside from Rosie O'Donnell).

Like other traits and cultures, you can stereotype sexual orientations all you want. Hell! It's fun to stereotype! And again, it's natural! The human brain chunks information together into schemas, so it's easier for our brains to hold vast amounts of information. But understand this: These thick blocks of information that we clump together in our heads will sometimes compel us to exclude applicable information. Because of this, schematizing makes it difficult to retain new information that does not conform to our already existing schemas. Therefore, it's important to continuously remind yourself to not judge and be open to every sexual orientation. *What, what!?!?*

REFERENCES:

1,500 animal species practice homosexuality. (2006, October 23). *Medical Science News.* Retrieved from http://www.news-medical.net/news/2006/10/23/20718.aspx

Adams, H.E., Wright L.W., & Lohr, B.A. (1996). Is homophobia associated with homosexual arousal? *Journal of Abnormal Psychology,* 105(3), 440-445.

Ciraldo, B., Swant, A. & Norman, S. (2007). What what (In the butt) [Recorded by Samwell]. On [www.youtube.com]. Milwaukee, WI: Brownmark Films.

Garcia, M. (2011, October). More Than Half of Women Attracted to Other Women. *Daily News.* Retrieved from http://www.advocate.com/news/daily-news/2011/10/20/more-half-women-attracted-other-women

Green, B.A. (2010). Understand schema, understand difference. *Journal of Instructional Psychology,* 37(2), 133-145.

Johnson, R.D. (2003). Homosexuality: Nature or Nurture [Supplemental material]. *AllPsych Journal.* Retrieved from http://allpsych.com/journal/homosexuality.html

McCann, P.D., Minichiello, V., & Plummer, D. (2009). Is homophobia inevitable? Evidence that explores the constructed nature of homophobia, and the techniques through which men unlearn it. *Journal of Sociology,* 45(2), 201-220.

Milar, K.S. (2011, February). The myth buster. *Monitor on Psychology,* 42(2), 24. Retrieved from http://www.apa.org/monitor/2011/02/myth-buster.aspx

Mitchell, J. C. (Producer & Director). (2006, October 13). *Shortbus* [Motion picture]. United States: THINKFilm.

Strong, B., Yarber, W.L., Sayad, B.W., & DeVault, C. (2008). *Human Sexuality: Diversity in Contemporary America* (6th ed.). Boston: McGraw Hill.

LOOK GUYS—BIG TITTIES!

"Look Guys-Big Titties!" is what I like to yell when I'm out with my guy friends and a girl walks in with an itty, bitty waist, and two round things in their face. They get sprung, to say the least. I'm also going to go out on a limb and say that when their attention is locked on a sexy woman with voluptuous breasts, I'm guessing the last thing on their mind is, "Is she a man?!?" But the truth is, you never know!

Unlike my said phrase from above, the true expression that the acronym "LGBT" has derived from is: Lesbian/Gay/Bisexual/Transgender. Some of you may have heard of this acronym with the extension, "Q", standing for "queer". This can sometimes be used as an umbrella term that covers lesbians, gays, bisexuals, transgendered folk, or questioning people, but is meant to be considered a separate identity all in itself. The reason why this "Q" is such a confusing concept for people to grasp a hold of is because they're intimidated to use the term. Is it offensive or complimentary? Well, according to who you ask, it's both; therefore, it's best not to call someone "queer", but if they identify themselves as queer, then accept and respect.

Talk about not labeling yourself with a pretty bold label! The reason why the word could possibly offend someone is because in the past, the word, "queer" was extremely derogatory. Nowadays, if people know that they are not heterosexual, but do not want to be described as a lesbian, gay, bisexual or transgendered person, they may label themselves as "queer". It's a kind of an "outside of the box" type of identification. The goal of using this term is to diminish the dichotomous labels and capture all of the possible sexual orientations, identities and practices that violate existing norms.

Confused? Well, according to our culture, so are transgenders. I mean, how many times did Mr./Mrs. Garrison undergo a sex change in the animated television series, *South Park*? Only Mr. Hat knows... No wonder our country has such a negative connotation associated with this term! The most well-known transgendered person is an animated character on *South Park*! What the hell ever happened to Rupaul?!?! The only famous cross-dresser that I know of is John Travolta, and even now his sexual excursions are confusing the shit out of me!

"I am who I am, who I am, well... Who am I?" Dave Matthews asks. I'm sure transgendered people can relate to this *Dancing Nancy* saying, considering the fact that some of them are known to ask the question, "What sex am I?"-a question most people don't have to ask twice. Talk about feeling uncomfortable in your own skin! A transgendered person is someone who feels comfortable as the opposite gender. There are many different variants along the transgender spectrum. Hell! Cross-dressing occurs every Halloween! But seriously, a man (gay or straight), may enjoy the feeling of his favorite silky, red bathrobe that he puts on every night before he goes to bed. A teenage girl may enjoy the attention she receives from putting a tie around her neck and dressing up more masculine on professional Fridays, or your dad may like wearing your mom's panties during church. Disgusting? Eh... To each their own. You like doing things to make yourself feel more comfortable and other people like doing things to make themselves feel more comfortable. As long as it wreaks no harm, no matter what these things are, everyone should have a right to do them to make their lives more comfortable.

Comfort. It's not considered a necessity of life, but it damn as well should be. Would you rather sleep on a bed or the hardwood floor? That's about as easy as the answer to whether you'd rather use your girlfriend's breasts as a pillow or a tortoise's shell? Come on… Everybody needs a bosom for a pillow, everybody needs a bosom! Well, as sucky as the downside to these preferences may seem, they're not half as bad as living a life wishing you were in a different body every minute of every day.

Gender Identity Disorder (GID) is recognized by the DSM-IV, and is commonly referred to as transexualism. You can kind of think of a transsexual as an extreme transgendered person. These are transgendered people who want to go through with surgery in order to physically change into the opposite sex. A female who wants to turn into a male is considered a trans man, and a male wanting to turn into a female is considered a trans woman. The first step people take when they are interested in this critical change is hormone pills/injections. And in order for them to do this, they must have a letter from a mental health professional (usually their personal therapist). To most trans people, the day they start their hormone therapy is the first day of their transition. Some may put that pill popping day up on the calendar and consider it a new anniversary; whereas, others may solemnly see it as the first day of a new beginning. Either way, depending on how far they want to go with their transition, they still have lot of work ahead of them.

During the hormone intake, trans people start to see changes. Their hair line realigns, their facial hair changes, and they get bigger *or* smaller. For most trans men, if they were considering keeping their breasts, after six months of a strong testosterone dosage they're begging their doctor to rip those puppies off! Why? It's because those hormones fuck with your brain!

One of the major confusions people have when it comes to transgender or transsexual people is their sexual orientation. Do not get confused, my Friends. Transgender people do not aim towards being the opposite sex for the pure satisfaction of having a "correct" sexual orientation. They want to change genders so their external selves match their internal selves. They want to look the way they feel. As for their sexual orientations... Well, it can be quite confusing. A straight man may be attracted to women, get a sex change and call himself a lesbian. A gay man may get a sex change and then call herself "heterosexual". But like I wrote before: Those hormones fuck with your brain! And sometimes the hormones change the object of the person's desire. Therefore, a gay woman who becomes a trans man may think that he will eventually be able to identify himself as "straight"; but, because of his hormones going haywire, he may have his sexual desire alter. Five years into the making, he may be fully transitioned into a man, and yet be attracted to other men-labeling himself, once again, as gay! Agh! I guess this is why they came up with the "queer" brand. Sometimes it's just easier that way...

Those who want to continue with the sex change will seek out sex reassignment surgery, now referred to as gender affirmation surgery (because you were always that gender, the surgery is now just affirming it-which I, personally, think is a really sweet way of titling it). Now, there are plenty of people who start the hormone process and do not continue with genital surgery. Genital reconstruction is not necessary for social gender recognition; and for many, it's not about the genitals. It's about how they walk around in the real world. They want to feel like they are in the right skin, and they want to appear that way to others too. In addition, it's extremely expensive and there are complications. For instance, there's a chance you could lose sensation. I don't know about you, but I'm not sure I'd risk my orgasms just so I'd look different down there!

The majority of the people who do have the lower surgery are trans women. This is because for trans men, the surgery is much more expensive, especially if they want their Cyclops well-endowed. But if they start saving, it's possible! It just may take anywhere between six to twelve surgeries until the final product is finished.

If they choose to have the lower surgery, they must get a second letter of recommendation written by another therapist. They also must live their life as the opposite sex for an extended period of time (~1 year). Tired yet? Well, there's more! In addition to the therapy, the hormones, and the gender affirming surgery-*just in case, the trans person still has some money left that they would like to blow*-they can continue forward with vocal cord surgery, breast surgery, tracheal surgery, nose surgery, facial reconstructive surgery, and don't forget legally changing their name! And the additional ~twenty-five bucks to alter their new driver's license?!?!? Thankfully, you can write that shit off! But don't think in a million years that you're insurance company is going to offer to pay for it!

Imagine spending your whole life trying to save up money just to put your body through the surgical stress so you feel "normal". These surgeries can total anywhere up to $250,000! Again... That's a pretty decent-sized house right there! Hell, I'd take that money and spend the rest of my days traveling the world! But not transsexuals. It's more important for them to feel like "normal" people feel every day. Talk about taking comfort for granted!

Whether a transgender or transsexual person has done whatever actions were necessary to make themselves feel "normal", they still have to deal with the reactions of every other person in their lives. A transgender child cannot make the decision to have gender affirming surgery until they are old enough. Instead, they take puberty blockers. This may make them feel safer and keep them from developing into a more complete form of a gender they do not want to be; but, think of how their peers will treat them. Delaying one's puberty is going to make them appear different than everyone else. And during the stage of adolescence, when you "look different" you become a target. As if they don't have enough on their plate already...

It doesn't get better with age either. Older, more mature, transgender people still have to pee! Now, when I go into the bathroom, the last thing I want to do is check out the other people who are in there. I want to run into my stall, do my stuff and get the hell out, in hopes of not breathing in anyone's shit smell. But, if I'm in there and a large, masculine figure walks into the room, I'm going to feel uneasy! It's just a natural reaction. But it sucks for her, if that's a trans woman, or simply a masculine woman. *Funny…* A trans woman walks into a bathroom, and catches the eye of another woman. The trans gets nervous, and feels judged because she knows she appears different than the other women entering the rest room. She thinks to herself, *Stop looking at me!* Whereas, the woman staring at her feels nervous as well. She feels insecure and possibly sexual harassed, thinking that this manly woman is possibly undressing her with her with her eyes. She has no clue that the large, intimidating woman feels just as uncomfortable as she does. Instead, she thinks to herself, *Stop looking at me!* Damn-it women! Stop looking at each other and RELAX!!! Just go do your shit! (Pun intended.)

REFERENCES:

Cornershop. (1997). Brimful of Asha. On *When I Was Born on the 7th Time* [CD]. London, England: Wiiija.

Dave Matthews Band. (1994). Dancing Nancies. On *Under The Table and Dreaming* [CD]. New York: Bearsville Studios.

Fetcho, R., "Tiny Tina". (2012, August 24). Interview by T. Puck [Phone conversation]. Cross dressers.

Giammattei, S. V. (2012, August 23). Interview by T. Puck [Phone conversation]. Transsexuals.

Sir Mix-A-Lot. (1992). Baby Got Back. On *Mack Daddy* [Tape]. Los Angeles: Def American Recordings.

The World Professional Association for Transgendered Health, Inc. (2012). Medical Necessity Statement. Retrieved from http://www.wpath.org/medical_necessity_statement.cfm

"HE" GAVE ME THE BEST ORGASM
OF MY LIFE!

W hy softball? Why can't girls play baseball? We're allowed
to play wiffle ball, basketball, volleyball, football, but never
baseball. Notice how the softball is much larger and harder to hit
further than a baseball. It's like we've been sabotaged so we can't
muscularly perform! Is this the real reason why George Hancock
created this sport? Because he was nervous? Perhaps the thought
of a woman dominating a man in America's sport made him panic-
stricken. So, he designed an "in-door" version of the sport, which
was designated to side-track women from overpowering the
men at their own game. They say women play this sport because
it's less physically demanding... Whatever... Like women can't
handle the speed of a small ball. If men truly didn't think women
could handle balls, they wouldn't be laying theirs in our eye
sockets and mouths every chance they had!

Whether you're a woman or a man, from the moment you
are born, you are exposed to both sex roles (which are biologically
determined), and gender roles (which are based on your femininity
and masculinity). Society expects you to follow accordingly. They
see gender as a binary term: If you're a woman, you should act
and do feminine things, and if you're a man, you should act and do
masculine things. So for instance, men work, women clean. Easy
enough, right? Men root for Eli or Peyton Manning, and women

root for Carrie or Sami Brady. Men "give it", and women "take it".
Wait a second...

These socially constructed roles deliver quite a bit of
mixed messages, don't you think? Luckily, as new generations
are introduced to these roles, they don't necessarily play by the
rules. Many women choose to take on various masculine roles
which allocate dominance and more power to them. At the same
time, society has created a safer space for any man who feels
comfortable acting in a more nurturing or gentle demeanor. If
you're imagining a flaming homosexual right now, stop being so
sexist! You may be 99% tomboy and 1% princess or vice versa.
Either way, you can't tell the sexual orientation of someone by the
gender or sex roles they play in society; otherwise, every time you
saw a housewife drag the garbage out to the curb, you'd think
she was a lesbian. And although *Desperate Housewives* would
have made it at least another five seasons if they were all having
hot, lesbian sex, the main characters were all straight... But, then
again... We all thought that about the *Sex in the City* characters,
and look what happened to Cynthia Nixon...

Like everything else in life, when it comes to gender roles, it
boils down to balance. Similar to how sexual orientation was once
viewed, masculinity and femininity were seen as opposite ends
of a dichotomy with no "in between". It wasn't until 1973 when
Anne Constantinople considered the idea that gender may be a
measureable variable with masculinity and femininity on either
end of the broad spectrum. Following up on Constantinople's
theory, Sandra Bem proposed that a balanced person who held
both masculine and feminine qualities may be a more happier
and well-adjusted person. As the idea was accepted, the term
androgynous (not to be mixed up with androgenous, which means
tending to produce male offspring) was coined.

When people hear of someone being described as
androgynous, they usually visualize a male with long rock star
hair, or a female with short hair, wearing jeans and a baggy

t-shirt, i.e. the girl from *Scary Movie* who played Sacha Baron Cohen's girlfriend in *The Dictator*. When describing someone as androgynous, the label isn't always assigned because of the physical appearance alone. It is extremely normal for people to act in an androgynous manner as well.

For instance, masculine personality traits are as follows: Aggressive, ambitious, independent, dominant, forceful, analytical, athletic, competitive, and individualistic. Feminine qualities can be listed as: Affectionate, cheerful, childlike, gullible, shy, warm, flatterable, compassionate and yielding. Are you offended by the sexism yet? Depending on the situation, people fluctuate between roles. A woman at work may act more self-sufficient than at home, because she knows her husband can take care of the more difficult tasks. A man may act more gentle and affectionate on a first date because he thinks it's what his date wants… Which brings us to the most complex concept. What are we attracted to?

A man wants a pretty lady in the streets and a sexy whore in the bedroom. A woman wants a good-looking asshole who can make her laugh, and provide. This brings up the old saying, 'You want what you can't have'. Notice how both the ideal woman and man have a pinch of sweetness to them and a dab of badass to them? The reality is, whether one wants the good girl with a splash of bad; or a nice guy with a dash of dick (pun intended), it's completely doable! That's why we have balance!

The good news? Finding that balance is an empowering thing! The bad news? It's fucking confusing! Let's talk feminism, shall we? A woman wants a man to make her feel like an equal. And he should! Not only can she attain an equally powerful and responsible job, education, and be as sexually aggressive; but, she can bear children as well! (All the power to us!) And yet, how many of you men have dated a woman who acts like that, but *still* wants you to pay for her dates, open the car door, and be her knight and shining armor!?! *What the fuck?!?!*

We are all human beings and pretty much capable of

doing the same thing. These roles displaying who unloads the dishwasher, who picks who up on a date, who manages the finances, or pays for the vacation does not determine how well shaped your relationship is. It may be perceived that way; but, a lot can be misread when one is judging a relationship based off of their roles.

A man may think that if his woman cooks for him, it's a sign that she loves and respects him; but, the reality may be that she hates his cooking. So, in order to ensure sanity to her taste buds she makes the meals. A woman may think if a man cleans out her car it's his way of telling her that he loves her; but the truth is that every time he sees her mess he gets annoyed. So, he cleans it to reduce his anxiety. These "signs of affection" can be sweet, but without proper communication these signs can also be a downward spiral that occurs due to the false sense of security. In the end, these relationships can best be described as nothing more than "routine".

If a man is not around, a woman is not going to let the trash sit and rot in her house. She's going to take it out! (Unless she's just *dirty*... And I'm not saying those filthy people don't exist... Cause they do... And they're disgusting...) And if a man's not around, a woman's going to get off! "'He' gave me the best orgasm of my life!?" Bullshit! The reality is: Those vibrators do things that **MAN** cannot do. And the same goes for men. When alone, they will masturbate, they will cook, and like the Italians, who prioritize their daily goals in the following order: "Gym. Tan. Laundry...", they *will* learn how to clean their own clothes. What about gay couples?!?! You think they rely on the opposite sex to fulfill their unassigned gender roles? Haha! They're the most self-sufficient of us all!

The construct of these gender roles ultimately mean nothing. The "fact" that boys own the color blue and girls look prettiest in pink has been culturally determined. But guess what?!?!? Just because the majority of our culture abides by these rules doesn't mean you have to! God bless America!

Personally, my favorite gender role argument is the act of sloring around. Culturally speaking, casual sex is only acceptable for men. I mean, Tucker Max made a whole career off of flaunting his sexual affairs... Although I challenge him... Want to compare stories and that determine who the more successful sexual conqueror is? Bring it on, Tuck!

REFERENCES:

About.com. (2012). Softball-George Hancock. Retrieved from http://inventors.about.com/library/inventors/blsoftball.htm

Bem, S. (1974). The measurement of psychological androgyny. *Journal of Consulting and Clinical Psychology*, 42(2), 155-162.

Cohen, S. C., Berg, A., Schaffer, J., Mandel, D., Hines, A., & Rudin, S. (Producers), & Charles, L. (Director). (May 16, 2012). *The Dictator* [Motion picture]. The United States: Paramount Pictures.

Gold, E. L. & Mayes, L. R. (Producers), & Wayans, K. I. (Director). (July 7, 2000). *Scary Movie* [Motion picture]. The United States: Dimension Films.

Maulding, R. (2012, September 30). Interview by T. Puck [Phone conversation]. Gender roles, Widener University.

Max, T. (2006). *I hope they serve beer in hell*. NY: Citadel Press.

Raymond, J. (Writer), & Kreisberg, B. (Director). (March 10, 2011). Gym, Tan, Find Out Who Sammi is Texting [Television series episode]. In Salsano, S., Jeffress, S., & French, J. (Producer), *The Jersey Shore*. Seaside Heights, NJ: 495 Productions.

Sensuality

This circle of sexuality revolves around our own experience with our bodies, as well as with others' bodies. Its major components include: Skin hunger, the human sexual response cycle, body image and fantasy.

ARE YOU SAYING I'M FAT?!?!

Depending on how one counts, there are over one hundred visible body parts of the human body. The chances that someone is satisfied with every single one is slim to none. Why?!? Well, because of *Barbie* of course! I mean, she was the closest thing to porn when we were children. No matter what sex or gender you identify as, one of your strongest memories of seeing the naked human form probably involved this doll. Now that's fucked up! And what's even more fucked up is the lasting impression it caused. Her body image has been etched into our brains as "normal". It doesn't matter that the dimensions of her body resemble a 5'9" tall woman, with a 39" bust, 18" waist, 33" hips and a size 3 shoe.

But sorry. You can't go around pointing fingers. If we're going to blame *Mattel* for providing girls with long-lasting body image issues, we're going to have to throw in some blame to *Hasbro*'s *G.I. Joe* and *Teddy Ruxpin* too! Cause he sure as hell did a job on *Ted*'s self-image!

For starters, according to the Centers for Disease Control, the average height of a female is 5'3". At this height, the average waist line is 37". As for the hip measurement? Well, according to research, men are most attracted to women who have a 0.7 waist to hip ratio (WHR). A woman with this measurement would be known to have an hourglass figure. Sorry to say, Ladies: You're born with your framework. So, you're going to have to deal with it. You may be pouting right now, because you think that everyone has an hourglass figure but you; but, here's a reality check for you: A study conducted at North Carolina State University found that ~46% of women were banana-shaped; over 20% were pear-shaped; ~14% were apple-shaped, and under 10% were hourglass-shaped. So if you resemble a fruit, don't fret! There are plenty of ways to camouflage your waist line to make you look more triangular. Just *Google* that shit (GTS)! And indulge yourself in a plethora of fashion websites trying to sell you their latest trends. OR… You could always be happy with what you have and flaunt the shit you were born with!

As for boobs? Again, GTS it, Girls. G-T-S! If you're not happy with your No-See-Um breasts, go buy some push-up bras and wear a V-neck shirt! There's a reason why *Victoria's Secret* has become the leading specialty retailer of lingerie in the United States. It's because they realized EVERY WOMAN has issues with their breasts! And I'm sad to report; it only gets worse as you age. Unlike men, whose dicks look the same at the age of 80 as they did when they were 20, a woman's breasts do not withstand time well.

It's not a shock to anyone that women place too much emphasis on comparing their bodies to others. You know when you're walking out of the grocery store, or down the street and other women are looking at you, giving you "the eye"? It's probably **not** because they're sexually attracted to you, but because they're sizing you up and comparing themselves to you. Again, it's fucked up. If a woman glances at you, and thinks you aren't as good looking as her, she'll actually get a burst of self-confidence. There are of course, exceptions to this. Secure women might size you up and compliment something about you to themselves. For instance, they may think after eyeing you, *Wow. She has beautiful highlights. I should ask her where she gets her hair done.* Or, *She is so beautiful. I wish I was that age again. She doesn't know how lucky she is.* (Usually, the older women are the more secure ones.)

As for men, when they are sizing each other up on the streets, they may be looking as vainglorious as women, and focus on the fashion and fitness; but, their observations usually build up to further speculations. A guy who is insecure and is walking past a good-looking guy will probably assume that the good-looking guy is a juice head and has a small dick. Or, if an insecure guy is walking past another man and his hot woman, the guy may deduce that the man only has that piece of ass because he's loaded. To make himself feel better, the next line in his head would probably be, *If I had his money, that girl would be mine... I bet I could kick his ass in a fight... Fucking loser....* For many men, it's not about the physical attractiveness; it's more about the competition of dominance. Who is the true alpha-dog? Then again, just like women, the more secure a man is in himself, the more polite his internal commentary may be when sizing up another man. If you are an Italian from the Jersey Shore, and a guy is walking towards you on the boardwalk, he may be thinking, *Wow. That guy is really fit! I really need to work out more...* But then, let's be honest with ourselves. You're an Italian... At the Jersey Shore... He's probably thinking, *Fucking Meathead. Go fist pump you're boyfriend's ass.*

Although 90% of people who suffer from an eating disorder are women, that doesn't mean that women are the only ones with body issues. Men have body issues too. The first one I would like to touch on, which goes for both men and women is the most ridiculous of them all. The obsession with skinny jeans:

Women are known to want to be smaller, and men are known to want to be bigger. But some men have a different vision of what's fashionable and sexy. These men usually describe themselves as "deep" and value being the "nice guy"; or on the other hand, act depressed and disappointed in the world. No matter what their philosophical view, these men and many women have this warped mind-frame that skinny jeans are hot! I'm only preaching the truth here: This generational obsession with these pants is a mistake! Haven't you ever seen your parents look at old photos and show disgust for something they've worn, or a hairstyle they've rocked when they were younger? One day, that will be you! Skinny jeans are the most horrendous craze ever invented. They taper to your ankle, the tiniest part on your leg. ANYONE who wears them is going to look large! Whether you're skinny-mini or have an apple-bottom ass, I'm telling you: You're going to regret wearing those pants, years to come. These hideous denims, which will NEVER make *anyone* look good, are called "skinny jeans". Complex, anyone?

Emoians are not the only males who have issues with their bodies. One that is not easily fixable is height. Men? I can't help you there. But what I can promise is that there are many women out there who prefer shorter men! Think about it! You can spoon correctly, fuck in the shower more smoothly, and every time you lean in for a kiss, she doesn't have to worry that you're hurting your neck from bending down! Also, it has a lot to do with their dads as well. If a woman has a healthy relationship with her dad, it has been ruled true that she will choose a man who is, in some ways, like her father. If the girl of your dreams has a dad on the shorter end of the stick, it may just luck out in your favor! Try to avoid wasting your dreams on undergoing limb extension surgery. You're more likely to find a mate if you take the $100,000 and make it a down payment on a nice house. Keep in mind; the average height for men is under 5'10". So, like women need to embrace the framework they were born with, you need to accept your stature. WARNING: The Napoleon Complex is one of the most annoying psychoses that **no** one is attracted to. Whether it's the height of your dick or the height of your body, if you come off as if you are "da shit", your arrogance will push people away faster than a city of Okies running from an F5!

Probably the main body issue young men have is weight-related. Yes, boys too, undergo fad-dieting, which is usually not nutritionally sound; and yes, boys are known to take steroids or other crap such as CytoSport's *Muscle Milk* and Creatine. Yet, four out of five men are unsatisfied with their muscleness. New research reveals that the number one body image issue that men have as they get older is a beer belly! If this is your secret qualm, here's a tip: Cut back on the binge drinking, Boys! Same goes for women!

*A general note here: When we were children, our drug of choice was sugar; but, the dosage of it was regulated by our parents (or at least should have been), which kept our weight down. Your R.A. in college is not going to stop you from doing keg stands to help you watch your figure. He or she's probably going to be the one dropping the beer into the three-story bong which will in turn add hundreds of calories to your body in less than three seconds! Are you a pothead? If so, you probably have a potbelly from the munchies, you high, little piglet. That'll do Pig! I SAID- THAT WILL DO! It's not calculus here, Kids. If you make these choices to put these drugs into your body, your body is going to respond by begging for food to balance things out. If you don't want to be overweight, don't overdo the drugs usage.

Finally, the genetic trait that few men can escape from is baldness. Although some studies say baldness is a recessive trait, two-thirds of men will develop some type of hair loss by the age of 60. "You can run, but you can't hide-"says the autosomal gene. Luckily, hair transplants are becoming more and more prevalent in modern society. Follicular unit micrografting is a method that involves taking hair from the back of someone's head and replacing the areas of baldness with the person's actual hair. This natural restoration approach has been going on for over thirty years and is a GREAT way to fill in the gaps when it comes to balding for both men and women. (Yes, up to fifty percent of women suffer from hair loss too!)

Alright, so it's obvious that both men and women have body issues. And the above information hasn't even touched on the subject. Like I wrote before, there are over 100 visible body parts.

People are going to have issues with specific bodily features. And I'm writing this chapter in hopes to normalize body image issues. They are just another challenge in life that everyone has to deal with. *How* you deal with them is the bigger issue.

You see, there are two types of body image issues: 1) Ones you can change, and 2) ones you can't. TayloR Puck's advice: Don't waste your time worrying about the ones you can't change. Waste your time learning to deal with them, and love them! There's nothing you can do about it. Stop focusing on something you can't change! As for the ones you can? FOCUS! And change them!

When it comes to body image issues, most sex educators will stand in front of you and blame *Mattel* for their faulty dimensions, and blame the media for exploiting only skinny-mini artists and buffed-up actors. I am here to state that if you are unsatisfied with your moobs, cottage cheese thighs, bird-cage chest, chewed up fingernails, hairy back, ratty hair or forehead's mustache-go fix it! Spend some time, money, and effort so you can feel healthy and happy again! I'm sure even Brad Pitt has to put some effort into looking good… Well, maybe not. But that's not the point! The rest of us all do!

Easier said than done? FUCK YEAH! Changing your lifestyle is hard. And unfortunately, very few people can do it at the drop of a *Yankee*'s hat. Why? Because they're not ready. But when their time comes; when that burst of motivation points them in the right direction, they'll be off! You've seen it before: A friend quits smoking-AND SUCCEEDS, your aunt goes on a diet-AND KEEPS THE WEIGHT OFF, your significant other and you start jogging every morning-AND A YEAR LATER YOU'RE BOTH PARTICIPATING IN A TRIATHALON! The hard part is finding the motivation to change. Another bit of TayloR Puck advice: Get rid of your TV. (It works.)

Battling your body image issues is physically hard enough. But, if you decide to take on the fight and begin to sense the taste of defeat, the change in your mentality will soon conquer all. Once you start appreciating your hard work, and notice the physical change in your body weight, reduction of the bags under your eyes, or glow of your skin, your emotions will have a positive change as well. It will be at this point in time, when you'll truly start loving the external AND internal "you". Sounds all good and swell; but, be patient! Life-changing alterations-especially falling in love with yourself take time… Possibly years! "It took me twenty-something years to learn how to love myself. I don't have that kind of time to convince someone else."

Focus on being healthy, and a sexier, happier new you will be a sure outcome. Here's a fact you can't deny: A healthy body is not a hideous body. So, the healthier you are, the happier you'll be. Again, unlike other sex educators who preach about body image issues, I would like to emphasize the three "H"s: Healthy, happy, and hot! Aim to be hot! Not cold! We are not penguins; nor whales. Antarctica is not inhabited by humans; therefore, the extra coat is blubber is unnecessary. Yes, it is natural and necessary to have body fat. It acts as a cushion for our organs, it assists in the maintenance in hormone production, and it provides large n' sexy tits and ass! Too much fatty deposits though can result in high blood pressure, high cholesterol, diabetes and heart attacks. And none of those medical conditions sound healthy, happy or hot…

Why am I enforcing the message of the three "H"s? When someone feels healthy, happy and hot, they have a higher chance of leading a more positive lifestyle. As a result, their confidence rises, their motivation soars, and their standards rise-for themselves, as well as others. In turn, the three "H"s improve the class of our entire society.

It takes sixty seconds or less for you to develop a first impression of someone. Your decision is based on features, such as appearance, posture, speech and demeanor. The first impression someone has of you is going to determine whether or not they are going to befriend you, agree to go out on a date with you, hire you, or give you a second a chance. When first impressions are cemented in, they are long-lasting, strong and hard to override.

But if you are a truly happy person you will exude positive energy. (Just don't be too cocky! Too much confidence will make you come off as if you love yourself, but may not result in being loved by all.)

They say you know when someone's in love with themselves if they doodle their name over and over again. It's like a girl who is constantly writing her first name and her boyfriend's last name all over her notebook. In this case, it's obvious that she's in love with the idea of "them". Another clue to know if someone's vain is if they tilt their chin down in photos, tilt their head to a fixed position, or purse their lips together-and actually look good. Why? Because those photogenic bastards have been practicing!!! As much as I hate these freakishly good-looking people in pictures, they have the right idea!

Learn how to become photogenic! Because the rule of thumb is: If you look good in pictures, you look good in real life. (Although, frequent online daters may debate on whether or not that's actually true.) You may think that the lower the number is on the scale-the hotter you are, but you are most certainly wrong. How does one become photogenic? I like to call it: Mirror Masturbation. Go make love to yourself in front of the mirror. It's as simple as that!

With forty-four muscles in your face, a human is known to be able to make up to 5,000 expressions. Some of these expressions are going to be attractive. Some will not. So, take some time and practice making faces at yourself. You might learn that your smile looks better when you pull the left corner a tad, or if you slightly squint your eyes a sex appeal that you never knew existed pops out from beneath your glare. Learn to loosen your shoulders and look less hunched over. Posture means everything! But remember, this new way of "getting off", just like the traditional masturbation act, gives you time alone with yourself. When you look at yourself in the mirror, focus on the beauty that you have to offer. Discover your highlights and learn to love yourself. And don't think that one or two looks is going to do it. Make this habit a daily ritual, and teach yourself how to look at others the way you look at yourself in the mirror. You may think that staring at yourself in the mirror is a vain practice (and it is), but would you rather be into yourself or not? I don't know about you, but I'm pretty sure Carly Simon was singing about me. Really… It's not that bad of a thing to be into yourself. Be positive and learn how to show off your looks! You are your worst critic, so if you can learn to attract yourself, you will come off as highly magnetic to others.

This habit only becomes dangerous if you choose to make love to yourself in your rearview mirror, which usually occurs with women. Eyes on the road, Little Lady! And we wonder why we have such a bad driving reputation…

But seriously, learning how to look good in front of a camera is a quick fix. A much more extreme "fix" requires a visit to the doctor's office.

People who have issues with their body, spend their time daydreaming about earning enough money to undergo surgery to change their physical appearance. Although there are times when this goal is acceptable, there are two other goals that one must meet before being able to appropriately follow through with cosmetic surgery. Goal #1: Be healthy. Goal #2: Be happy. These are two very effortless and broad terms, but the magnitude of attaining both is ultimately life changing. If you have *serious* body issues, the chances that you are both healthy and happy are quite slim. And the truth of the matter is that once you achieve both of these goals, you probably won't even want to continue any further with body reconstruction. The reason is because when you are both healthy and happy, you think differently. You view yourself differently and you learn to accentuate your fine points and douse your flaws. Am I repeating myself here?

The only type of cosmetic doctor that our country finds socially acceptable for young people to visit is the orthodontist. Since this is the case, my advice to anyone who has the money for to fix their appearance is to GO GET BRACES! One of the factors that determine class is straight teeth. And what's one of the first things people notice about you? Your smile! (In other words-your teeth.)

Sure braces cost thousands of dollars! But they're a lot less expensive than a brand new set of titties or labiaplasty! First impressions start at the eyes and then the mouth. We are taught that a good first impression starts with eye contact, followed with a smile. The eye part is easy because… Well, who doesn't have beautiful eyes? (Note to girls: When you hear a guy compliment the beauty in your eyes, feel free to roll them. What? Can't he come up with anything better than that? Note to boys: Everyone has beautiful eyes. If you want to compliment the one you're with, try to be a bit less cliché with your flattery remark.) So, if you can help it, you want to make that smile a beautiful one too.

Now that I've given you a complex about your teeth… Take your time. Figure out what you want to change about yourself- IF ANYTHING-and figure out a *healthy* way to do it! Whether the front of your neck makes you look like you're staring at someone from behind a pile of pancakes, or the back of your neck looks like a package of hotdogs, there are ways to avoid making people think that you use a mattress for a tampon. Recognize the fact that EVERYONE has these issues. The truth is: One day, you'll look back on this time and wish you were as fat or as ugly as you think you are now, because as you age your teeth get yellower, and everything starts to head south. Enjoy what you have now. Time is a real motherfucker.

REFERENCES:

Bell, S. A. (2012). Do women go bald? Retrieved from http://ezinearticles. com/?Do-Women-Go-Bald?&id=1473023

Kopinsky, S. (2012). Baldness gene. Retrieved from http://www.newton. dep.anl.gov/askasci/mole00/mole00480.htm

Leviticus, J. (2010). Facts about balding. Retrieved from http://www. livestrong.com/article/87210-balding/

Marcia, H. P. (2003, November 13). South Florida Sun-Sentinelbusiness strategies column.

McClatchy Tribune Business News. Retrieved from http://0-search. proquest.com.libcat.widener.edu/docview/461402228?accountid=29103

Marsh, L. (2011, April 14). Life-size Barbie gets real women talking. *NBCNews.com.* Retrieved from http://today.msnbc.msn.com/ id/42595605/ns/today-today_news/t/life-size-barbie-gets-real-women-talking/

McCormack, H. (2005, November 21). The shape of things to wear: Scientists identify how women's figures have changed in 50 years. *The Independent.* Retrieved from http://www.independent.co.uk/news/ uk/this-britain/the-shape-of-things-to-wear-scientists-identify-how-womens-figures-have-changed-in-50-years-516259.html

McDowell, M. A., Fryar, M. S., Ogden, C. L., & Flegal, K. M. (2008). *Anthropometric reference data for children and adults: United States, 2003-2006* (NH Publication No. 10). Retrieved from http://www.cdc.gov/nchs/ data/nhsr/nhsr010.pdf

Medical Xpress.com. (2012). Beer belly is biggest body issue for men. Retrieved from http://medicalxpress.com/news/2012-01-beer-belly-biggest-body-issue.html

Pampered Passions. (n.d.). Victoria's Secret, a brief history. Retrieved from http://www.pamperedpassions.com/victorias-secret-brief-history

PR. Newswire. (2012, April 19). First impressions are everything: New study confirms people with straight teeth are perceived as more successful, smarter and having more dates. Retrieved from http://0-search.proquest.com.libcat.widener.edu/docview/1002555722?account id=29103

Silva, M. (2006). Body image dissatisfaction: A growing concern among men. Retrieved from http://www.msoe.edu/life_at_msoe/current_student_resources/student_resources/counseling_services/newsletters_for_mental_health/body_image_dissatisfaction.shtml

Simon, C. (1971). You're So Vain. On *No Secrets*. [Audio Cassette]. London: Trident Studios. (1972).

ARE YOU HUNGRY FOR MORE?

Y ou're lying face down, naked on the table, trying to relax and focus on your breathing. You continuously adjust your face in the circular pillow in hopes to find the perfect position. In the background, you hear soft sounds of a waterfall, as if you were alone in a Hawaiian rainforest. As you focus on the liquefied resonance and your air intake, you ponder over the fact that the water sound is not generating a need to urinate. You smile because you are grateful; you're too comfortable to move now. You take another breath. *Uh oh*, you think. *I need to pee.*

Your thought dissolves when you perceive the door is opening. Someone enters the room. You hear the sink turn on. *Damn… I JUST PEED TEN MINUTES AGO! WHAT THE HELL?!?* The sink shuts off, and you listen to the soft sounds of hands being patted down on a fluffy towel. This is followed by a smacking, wet sound which makes you laugh to yourself. *He, he, he… Sounds like SOMEONE'S waxing the dolphin!* A hint of eucalyptus hits your nostrils, and a calming sense takes over as you hear the person position themselves above your dorsal body cavity. You feel the temperature of the lotion increase as they slide their cool, creamy hands down your back. *Mmm… IT FEELS SO GOOD!*

Whether or not your massage ends in a happier ending than Osama bin Laden's death, you can rest assure that your body will receive plenty of attention and your hunger pangs will be satisfied.

Skin hunger pangs, that is! But, before I go on describe what the hell skin hunger actually is; I'm going to focus on a TayloR Puck segment to resolve all of the unanswered questions that hover in young people's minds regarding the massage world. Please bring your attention to:

The Etiquette of a Happy Ending

When fighting with one's best friend, their right hand, sometimes one yearns for variety. In this case, they usually go to their significant other; but, if that is not an option for you, you may look elsewhere. Prostitution is always available, but illegal in all states except for some counties in Nevada, and NO-Las Vegas is not in one of these. Indoor prostitution was also legal in Rhode Island because of some loophole the hookers jumped through, but they closed that hole in 2009. But surprising enough, receiving a happy ending in a massage parlor is not socially accepted as a form of prostitution. Why? Because by using ambiance and medical licenses, massage parlors have warped paid sexual gratification into an erotic and exotic experience! And because there are also loopholes that the massagers have learned to jump through.

For one, even though happy endings are known to happen on cruise ships, and in commercial massage spas, it is speculated that the majority of happy endings occur at Asian massage parlors, or how older and politically incorrect people like to call them, "Oriental massage parlors". You can even tell by the advertising that the Asian parlors use; such as "Young Asians" and "China Doll Massage" that they are selling more than just a body massage; but, the attractive, young Asian women, as well. It's not that these whordorable women are actual whores! I mean, some *might* be... But these women have chosen a career in massage, and a lot of them purely get professional fulfillment from helping others relieve stress and be happier through the sense of touch. And for some, if that consists of sexual release, they will be willing to help! Some come from a culture where when you receive a body massage, you receive a *full* body massage; and that includes the genitalia. As for our country, it's more "hush-hush".

When asking for a happy ending, you don't just come out and inquire about "getting fucked", "getting a BJ", or "getting a hand job". It's more of an unspoken query. A slight touch on her arm, side or back can let her know that you're sincere, gentle, and wanna fuck. Or, when you turn right-side up, while claiming that it's hot, you can ask if it's alright if you remove your towel. If she gives you permission, and the result is a naked man lying there, blue steel and all, she'll get the picture. Verbal queries are usually shied away from; unless you're going to guide her to the areas where you hold the most amount of tension: your lower abdomen or your upper thigh. If you do conjure up the courage to bluntly ask after pitching a tent for some extra genital love, you might simply say, "Can you help me out?" Although, that gives way for verbal rejection, and a possible law suit; so, I wouldn't recommend it.

As for pricing, it's also not usually spoken about. When visiting a massage parlor or spa, you aren't visiting a brothel. Tip! AND TIP WELL! None of this twenty dollar bullshit! She's not a server bringing you *Patron* shots, shots, shots, shots, shots, shots, shots, shots, shots, shots, shots, shots, shots, shots, shots, shots! She's physically and mentally exerting herself to do something that possibly no other person wants to do; remember-you're paying for this because you couldn't get it for free! Head for the hundreds! And if fifty's the best you can do, slam it on top of the original twenty she should be getting for the body massage in the first place. "Why not ask how much?" you may wonder. Because that's prostitution, dumbass! Depending on the licenses these girls have and what state they're working in, if giving verbal confirmation to the wrong dude, they could get arrested for either a misdemeanor or a felony. If it's all non-verbal, she could possibly allege that she thought they had a personal connection and became sexually physical with no intentions of asking for money. The majority of the time, they just play dumb; and act like they don't speak English.

Finally, the question that is on every girl's mind right now is: What about girls? Yes, Ladies. Girls get their fun too. It's just less common, but not necessarily uncommon to find a hot masseur to rub you right. Just ask around. If you ask a masseuse for the number of a hottie masseur, because you're "too busy to travel to the spa", and need someone with extra muscles to come to your house to relieve the "extra tension" you've gained from the office, they'll get the picture and recommend someone who will do the trick. And for all of you Rhode Islanders out there, if he comes to your home, you can take a risk and just be blunt! "You're in my house now, Bitch!"

For those of you non-heteros, there's no extra challenge for you. Some masseuses relieve sexual tension for women; as well as masseurs do the same for men. Just ask around and you'll get references and all of the information: whether the massager will perform assplay, use his/her mouth, or just give a simple lotianic massage. Just remember: No matter what rating your happy ending gets, use a condom!! And try to refrain from insulting your massager and getting arrested. Just be subtle, and if it doesn't happen, get the hint.

For people who enjoy body massages, hugs and other forms of being physically touched, they are known to have high skin hunger. Humans actually receive messages as a result from their physical body responding to them. This physical sensation will have a negative effect on one's emotions if the body is feeling a lack of another human's touch. The comfort of another human's touch doesn't necessarily have to be sexually stimulating; it could result from butt pat that occurs after a kickoff, or teamwork exercise that requires group entanglement, or a hug from a best friend, or the nestling of a baby into its mother's breast. Whether you're a senior citizen with Alzheimer's disease or a newborn; as said by Australian sexpert, Rosie King, "Skin hunger is with us from the cradle to the grave."

Even research on preterm neonates, attests that prenatal babies who are handled and massaged more, maintain a healthier weight, and act much more calm and less irritable state than babies who are not physically held as much. This should not act as a surprise to anyone who is accustomed to witnessing a caring mother and her infant. Although, here's some food for thought: If breastfeeding is considered a sexual act, which it is; then, is breastfeeding an incestuous act? He, he he… And you thought only West Vigianians did that shit!

For those of you who are in sexual relationships with another/other people, it is important to recognize your level of skin hunger, as well as your partner's('). Just because your best friend reports that she's licked every part of her boo's body, doesn't mean she is actually satisfying his skin hunger. As much of a pussy John Mayer actually is, he has earned his fame by writing one of the popular songs that every girl wants to have sex to: "Your Body is a Wonderland". The most powerful line? "Discover me, discovering you".

Well-known erogenous zones, such as the ears, behind the knees, the ass and inner thighs will make one cringe in delight when touched. But just because a part of the body is not labeled as "erogenous" doesn't mean it can't be. Think back to a time, when someone has glided their fingertip along your forearm; whether your mother or your lover. If you felt as though your skin was sizzling with sensual fire, then you have a high level of skin hunger. Quite in the opposite, if you pulled your arm away in shock and became annoyed that someone touched you without permission, you can assume that your skin hunger registers on the lower level.

Being in a relationship with someone who has a different level of skin hunger than you can be challenging. If you have a high level and your partner is ok with being the giver during foreplay, it could possibly work out in your favor. But one TayloR

Puck exercise that I would like to share with you is the "Tracing of the Body". Recall the sensation of the fingertip on your forearm. Now, imagine that fingertip being dragged along your entire body. The "Tracing of the Body" is when one partner lies down naked and the other takes their time dragging their fingertip along the largest organ on their body: their skin. There is no time limit, and since it promotes relaxation, and takes such little energy on the tracer's part, they are happy to exert the time and energy into the exploration. During this exercise, remember to communicate the areas of high sensitivity, so your partner knows which ones to return to in the future. Asking for extra affection in certain areas of your body is not a crime! And remember to have fun, and RELAX! This exercise also helps people overcome their body image issues with their partners; as they are encouraged to lie still and expose their naked selves to their significant other.

*This certainly feels better if the person has long nails and can use the tip of the nail alone; but, a side note to men: Women appreciate men with short fingernails. If you are a guitar player, know that picks were created for a reason. In your case, you probably aren't getting many dates because of that one long fingernail you refuse to cut because you feel as though you couldn't rock the riffs without it. You choose: Either cut the nail, or you'll be playing your own instrument… Solo.

An UNrecommended way to explore skin hunger is to do drugs. But refer to your health facts, Kids: Drugs are bad, m'kay? Not only are they bad, but ecstasy is known to be one of the most dangerous drugs that young people experiment with today. Ecstasy (MDMA) is an amphetamine in pill form that fucks with serotonin levels; which in turn, fucks with your brain. Whether you choose to take the drug orally or shaft it up your ass, you're going to experience some shady side effects. Yes, this "love drug" is known to make people happy and very touchy-feely, but short term effects consist of confusion, depression, lack of sleep, anxiety and paranoia. Not to mention the long-term effects which include degradation of the brain, leading to memory loss. Another drug that is known to have a similar effect on serotonin like ecstasy does is bath salts. But no matter how masochistic your partner is; I'm pretty sure that if you start gnawing away at their face, it's going to take away from the skintastic pleasure you were originally aiming for. (And yes, I know that they determined that the 'Miami Zombie' was not on bath salts at the time of his cannibalistic feast, but that classic current event was definitely the meal that put bath salts on the map.)

Whichever way you receive extra skintalating stimulation, for people who have high levels of skin hunger and who acquire high amounts of skin sensation, they are known to be more content, more alert and better communicators. But what about those who have low levels of skin hunger? These people are usually those who have grown up in abusive homes, were deprived of touch from their parents while growing up or have had negative relationships in the past. For instance, if a woman has been in a relationship where the only time her man touched her was when he was indicating that they were about to get physical, she may become accustomed to associating a simple touch with a negative response. It takes time and *healthy* relationships to follow, in order for someone to heal from a damaged reaction to skin hunger.

If you find yourself in a relationship with someone that doesn't appreciate your touch, have no fear! There are ways to improve their desire to be touched by another. A quick test would be to find out if they would value a professional massage (with or without a happy ending). If their answer is, "No," then try to entice them with a couple's massage and do your best to place the focus on the two of you experiencing pleasure together; rather than placing the emphasis on their massage alone.

You can also suggest a hand job. And what I mean by that is a pedicure. Pedicures will leave your partner's hands sparkling, as well as give them bouts of mini hand massages. This way, you are starting off small; and they will soon learn to familiarize themselves with the pleasure that is received when someone is massaging a part of their body.

Sometimes adding a third party to the picture isn't the best route to go. If your partner is willing to explore skin hunger, but through your guidance only, there are techniques the two of you can try in order to make the experience smooth and enjoyable. Remember TayloR Puck's touch modality exercise: the "Tracing of the Body", and let the goosebumping begin! Also, there are films to give you more direct advice. One, in particular, which is highly recommended, is *Sensate Focus* films. These films provide therapeutic counseling for you and your partner. Real couples perform in the films, and as you progress through the erotic and energizing steps, both you and your partner will experience positive energy as you take on the journey of body exploration.

REFERENCES:

American Council for Drug Education. (2001). Basic facts about drugs: Ecstasy. *American Council for Drug Education.* Retrieved from http://www. acde.org/common/ecstasy.htm

Anonymous. (2012). *A Happy Ending/Interviewer: TayloR Puck.*

Black, J. (2006). Internet and multimedia review: The joy of erotic massage. *Sexual and Relationship Therapy*, 21(1), 117-118.

Craig, A.D. (2003). Interoception: The sense of the physiological condition of the body. *Current Opinion in Neurobiology*, 13, 500-505.

DiSalvo, D. (2012). The Straight Dope on What Bath Salts Do to Your Brain and Why They're Dangerous. *Forbes.* Retrieved from http://www.forbes. com/sites/daviddisalvo/2012/06/05/the-straight-dope-on-what-bath-salts-do-to-your-brain-and-why-theyre-dangerous/

Philips, R.B., University Medical Ctr., Early Intervention Program, Jacksonville, FL US, Moses, H.A. (1996). Skin hunger effects on preterm neonates. *Infant-Toddler Intervention*, 6(1), 39-46.

Prostitution. (2010). *ProCon.org.* Retrieved from http://prostitution. procon.org/view.resource.php?resourceID=000119

Sensate Focus. (n.d.) *COSRT.* Retrieved from http://www.cosrt.org.uk/pdf/ sensate_focus.pdf

Skin Hunger. (n.d.) *Extendicare.* Retrieved from http://www. extendicarecanada.com/uploads/public/53/docs/skin%20hunger_Jul%20 06.pdf

SHOW ME YOUR "O" FACE

Oh, oh, oh, it's magic! You know! Whether or not orgasms are what E.L.O. or Selena Gomez were referring to, I like to think so. Because personally, I think orgasms are-oh, oh, oh, *so* magical. And so do a shitload of other people. Enough to have a shitload of research executed on the subject.

For every action, there is a reaction. And when something sexually stimulating happens, a sexual response occurs. The human sexual response cycle is the series of physical and emotional changes that occurs when a person undergoes a sexual act, i.e. intercourse or masturbation. And let me tell you-it's fucking awesome!

If asked to describe the human sexual response cycle, most of you would probably bullshit some vague description that somewhat resembles John Bancroft's "psychosomatic circle of sex". His schema describes the act of sexual response. He basically said that humans cognitively process an erotic stimulus, which tells the limbic systems and other parts of the brain to get ready for sex. Then, the spinal cord and nerves get involved, and send messages to the genitals. Afterwards, the body gets prepared all over again. I like to think of the whole communication system like the Morse code, where nerves are constantly tapping the message throughout the body, "*It's sexy time!*"

Now Bancroft's circle is correct. But there is much, much

more that goes on when we are sexually active. The most important thing to know about the sexual response cycle is that everyone responds differently. *Duh.* This may seem obvious to you, but because people fail to remember this in the bedroom, sexual dysfunctions occur. Most people are not in tune with their body, or their partner's(s'), while they are in the act of nookie; therefore, if everything doesn't go exactly as erotically planned, they freak out. For instance:

You're having sex with your girlfriend in your bedroom. The television's on to drown out the creaking noise your springs are making while you hump away. You have her one leg up in the air, and the other between yours. Even though you're looking at her, you're concentrating on the sounds from the hallway, hoping that your parents don't walk in on you.

You keep going in and out of the zone; trying to get close to cumming, but holding back because you don't want to finish until she does. You have anxiety regarding your parents, stimulation on your dick, a hot visual of your girlfriend's tits, and every twenty seconds get a little gist of the commentary on the *A&E Ancient Aliens* episode. You're all over the place, but the most important thing in your head is trying to get your girl to cum (so she reports positive things to her bffs in school the next day).

The two of you have locked eyes and you're listening to her moan quietly. This continues for over five minutes and you start to realize that you're sweating profusely. *Is she close?* you think to yourself. She keeps looking you dead in the eyes. "Oh......oooh...." *Yeah, Baby. You like my shit*—you assure yourself. *You're close. I can see it in your eyes.* Her moaning gets a tad louder. You contemplate on whether or not to put your hand over her mouth, but decide not to because her increase in volume is bringing you to a climax. Then, all of a sudden, she turns her head quickly towards the television and says in a quirky voice, "What?" She looks back at you and says, "Do you believe that?"

You stop pumping. "Believe what?" you ask, panting

desperately.

"Do you believe that aliens built the pyramids?" she asks you in a more serious tone of voice.

You look at her in disbelief. *What the fuck!?!?*

According to the *Elvis Duran and the Morning Show* debate, women get tired of sex that extends past thirteen minutes (this does not include foreplay or afterplay). Although many women agree with this testimony, "boredom" is not necessarily the best, nor the nicest way to put it. Is it possible you're lady became bored? Sure! But I'd rather say that she just got lost somewhere along the plains of her sexual plateau.

Ever hear of Masters and Johnson? William H. Masters and Virginia E. Johnson were the two masterminds behind the human sexual response cycle. I'm sure they had plenty of fun researching the cycle, considering Will left his wife for Virginia. "Hi, Honny. No, I won't be home for dinner tonight. Virginia and I just stumbled across some amazing data! We're going to be up all night researching."-Yeah, and don't read into the fact that minus a couple of "i"s, and an "r", add an "a", and the woman's name consists of both male and female genitalia. (It's like she was born to master the art of boot knocking!)

Anyway, Masters and Johnson's version of the human response cycle consists of four stages: excitement, plateau, orgasm & resolution. A woman named Helen Singer Kaplan was unsatisfied with this four part method. She argued that Masters and Johnson's steps were only physiological responses and that the human sexual response cycle could not exist without being jumpstarted by desire. So, she added "desire" as a first step to the cycle to integrate the psychological aspect of getting "turned on".

Now when you add all of these together, you come up with five distinct phases that the body undergoes during a sexual encounter. Although these stages are not clearly demarcated from each other, you will recognize some of the physiological responses as you read through the following:

❶ Desire—"I need to get laid." Desire is the stage where you recognize that you either want to be romantically or sexually involved with another person. This sexual cognitive process is commonly associated with the sluttiest of the deadly sins: Lust. It is at this point, before the physical aspect kicks in, that someone becomes psychologically interested in sex; eventually, and hopefully, leading to physiological arousal.

Although this stage is *desirable* for many, it is not absolutely necessary to get to the next sexual response level. People who are involved in unfavorable sexual acts, can still experience physiological changes from the succeeding sexual response levels. For example, a woman who is in a relationship with a man who won't let her have a good night sleep until he receives his nightly blow job, might get tired of being poked religiously in the lower back even though she has made it quite clear that she's tired and uninterested. She may begin the sexual act without any feeling of desire whatsoever; but, will probably experience bodily changes from the subsequent stages. If you are smirking to yourself right now because this sounds like you and your girl, wipe your fucking face. Stop **making** your girl give you sex. It's not necessarily called "rape", but it's *not* too far-fetched from the abhorrent act. Either wait for her to do it when she wants to do it, or move on to someone else. Making a girl go down on you is a demeaning and derogatory act. If she's not in the mood, don't push.

❷ Excitement—"Mmmm...." The excitement stage can last ten to thirty seconds and up to a few hours, after experiencing the sexual stimuli. In this stage, you begin to feel and see your actual body change. Your muscle tension begins to increase, your heart rate and breathing increase as well, your nipples become hard and erect, you receive excess blood flow to the genital area, and a sex flush may appear. (This cute, little mannerism that your skin undergoes is a pinkish glow that appears on your chest and back and other areas of the body; it's as if your body is blushing from the x-rated act that it is about to partake in.)

Men take note that their testicles swell, their scrotum tightens, their dick begins to grow larger and harder. While these penile changes are physically visible, what might not be so noticeable is the lubricating liquid that is brewing inside.

As for females, their breasts become fuller (yay for A cups!), their vagina becomes lubricated, and their clitoris, labia majora, and labia minora all begin to swell. What's not so noticeable is that her vaginal walls begin to swell, and the vagina actually lengthens and expands.

Wait a second…why is the vagina undergoing so many internal changes? You may ask. Because it's preparing for pregnancy! Yup! Even at the excitement stage, it's goal is to get ready, in hopes that some guy shoots a healthy load at the right time of her menstruation cycle. (Better use a fucking condom! That's all I have to say!)

❸ **Plateau**—"Don't stop!" This intensified excitement stage can either be the most fun part, or the death of a sexual experience. The traits from the last stage are exaggerated; so, the muscle tension, sex flush, breathing, heart rate, and blood pressure continue to increase. Muscles spasms begin to occur in the feet, hands, and face.

It is at this point, one can truly determine if the man is well-endowed or not. During the plateau, the penis reaches its full erection. Quite the opposite, the testes appear smaller because they climb up, close to the scrotum. (Some say this helps the man look even bigger!)

The vaginal lips become puffy and turn a dark purplish color; somewhat resembling the girl who turns into a blueberry in the Willy Wonka movie. The clit becomes extra sensitive, and as if it's hiding from too much pleasure, it takes cover under the hood.

The plateau stage can last for hours, and is the leading way to the big "o". This stage can be tricky, since the majority of the time, both partners (or in some cases, multiple partners), are thirsting for the next stage but normally reach it at different times. Men can easily cum within two minutes of being physically stimulated, whereas women seem to take much longer; hence, the common task men must master: Sidetracking their brain, in order to keep themselves from cumming.

Is there a trick to this task? There sure is! Instead of thinking of baseball, your grandmother, or dying kittens, just relax and have fun! If you sense that you or your partner is getting lost along the plains, refocus what you're doing and change it up a bit. Don't fret! Use eye contact, touch different areas, and most importantly communicate. They'll let you know what they need in order to make it to the next level. Once excess excitement is present, you'll be ready for the climax.

❹ **Orgasm**—"Oh my God!" The big "o". This mind-boggling experience is unfortunately, the shortest of the phases. Once again, blood pressure, heart rate, and breathing all increase, as the body requires a rapid intake of oxygen. The feet become overwhelmed with tremors, and sex flush appears galore! At the moment when the orgasm is triggered, both myotonic and vascular responses occur in both bodies; in other words, changes are occurring in the muscle contractions and blood vessel flow._

Men come to the conclusion that they are "going to blow" because seminal fluid collects in their urethral bulb. Then, due to contractions in the base of the penis, they are able to ejaculate-all over one's face, in a vagina, in an ass, or in a sock.

The first third of the woman's vagina begins to contract rhythmically every ~8/10 of a second. The uterus also contracts in hopes to help aid the sperm on their race to the egg. (Again, if you're just looking for a good fuck with no embryonic development to follow, note that your bodies are really working against you, so *please* use a damn condom!)

The orgasm can be quite the pickle! The three pieces of

anatomy that people speculate are needed in order for one to experience an orgasmic burst are genitalia and the central nervous system (the brain and spinal cord); however, this is not always the case. Going back to Bancroft's "psychosomatic circle of sex", these three body parts are constantly communicating with each other in order to allow the body to experience the sensational blow. And if it were that easy, scientists would be able to explain the process of an orgasm with no problem. But what about a quadriplegic, who can get off? How about an amputee who claims he feels orgasms in his missing foot? Because of these abnormalities, it is obvious that genitals-to-spine-to brain is not the only orgasmic route! As scientists continue to unravel the enigma of the orgasm, it is clear to say, this climatic event is extremely complex.

Now the quote, "I don't trust anything that bleeds for a week and doesn't die", is said by many men. It is obvious that for most, if they had the choice of choosing their gender, they would choose to keep the dick and pass on the pussy. Another bonus that men have is the fact that they don't have to deal the pain of pulling one's upper lip up, over, and around their head; in other words, childbirth. On the contrary, women do have a benefit hidden up our sleeves. We may have to bleed once a month, **BUT** we get more intensified orgasms!

I'm not even going to bother throwing out a percentage on how many women can or cannot have orgasms, because depending on which study you find, it's a different statistical number every time. What I will say is that there are some women who claim that they cannot orgasm. But one thing is for certain: There is a LARGE amount of women who cannot orgasm through coital stimulation alone. Luckily, God has blessed women with the little man on the boat, which looks a bit like the button mouse imbedded in older laptops. So women?!?! Be glad you live in America, and it's not a cultural tradition to receive a clitoridectomy-removal of the clitoris. Ouch!

The reason for existence of the clitoris has not been proven, but one thing's for sure: **Proper stimulation** will produce fireworks…. Literally. If one's brain is observed through an MRI scanner during an orgasm, the brain lights as if it's Christmas. So, when people say 'their brains switch off' when they reach the big 'O', it's a crock of shit. The brain does the opposite. It turns on, full-speed! Theta waves that have been measured in the brain while a person orgasms are ten times stronger in a woman than a man. If the amount of theta waves correlates to the intensity of the orgasm (which is hypothesized), than women's orgasms are ten times stronger than a man's! Some scientists have even conjectured that if a man were to experience a woman's orgasm, it could possibly kill them. I think that's a bit far-fetched, though.

In a nutshell, when trying to bust a nut, don't race to the finish line! Because in reality, there's not always going to be a triumphant ending; although, that doesn't mean you both (or all) can't be winners! If lucky enough to experience an orgasm, I assure you, you will enjoy the euphoric state. Other physiological releases that can be compared to this occurrence are sneezing, and the act of a well-needed excrement. But I'm sorry… I'd take a good orgasm over a sneeze, or a good shit, any day! Keep in mind; it is during this stage in which one is explicably labeled as a moaner, talker, screamer or all three. He, he, he…

❺ **Resolution**—"I love you." This is the stage where the body heals from the high, and returns to its normal level of functioning. Swellness fades, body parts return to their normal positions, and original body color reappears.

In addition to men's weak orgasms, another downside is revealed in this stage: The refractory period. Depending on the age and health of the man, he has to wait for a period of time after each orgasm, before he can experience another. Women, on the other hand; if able to have another, "Oh, oh, oh…", will probably choose to go, go, go… Again. Don't feel bad if your woman is still thirsty for more and your cock is out of order. That's why God blessed you with a back-up! The strongest muscle in your body: Your tongue.

WOMEN BEWARE: At this stage, a large level of oxytocin, the "love hormone", is released into both men and women. Women also have large influxes of this hormone in scenarios; such as giving birth, breast-feeding, and maternal behaviors. On the other hand, men don't have as many case scenarios when their body is filled with this love-inducing hormone. Since this is the case, after they do orgasm, they are known to be exceptionally vulnerable-and sometimes say things "in the heat of the moment". Out of the **large** amount of men who think to themselves after a good orgasm from a woman, *I think I love you*, a small percentage actually slip and say it aloud. Some TRP advice: If the **first** time your man says, "I love you" is after an orgasm, don't take it seriously.

Back to the case scenario. Sex isn't always going to be perfect. Just focus on having fun and being safe! When you really get to know someone, you may find yourself having a full blown conversation and laughing out loud while you're riding each other. If experiencing the awkward opposite, perhaps two (or three, or four) of you aren't ready to share the full sexual experience just yet. No matter what, sex is suppose to be an intimate experience between you and your partner(s), so focus on the connection between your bodies. Next time you boink a loved one (or fuck buddy), focus on your human sexual response cycle. Focus on your partner's(s') too. You'll learn a lot about each other, and your connection will continue to grow.

References:

Abraham, R.A. (2010, March 4). Your Guide to the Sexual Response Cycle. *WebMD*. Retrieved from http://www.webmd.com/sex-relationships/guide/sexual-health-your-guide-to-sexual-response-cycle

Elvis Duran and the Morning Show. Premiere Radio Networks. Z-100, New York. Radio.

Kaplan, H.S., Horwith, M. (1983). *The Evaluation of Sexual Disorders: Psychological and Medical Aspects*. New York: Brunner/Mazel.

Margulies, S. & Wolper, D. L. (Producers), & Stuart, M. (Director). (June 30, 1971). *Willy Wonka & The Chocolate Factory* [Motion Picture]. United States: Wolper Productions.

Marshall, M. (2009). Six things science has revealed about the female orgasm. *New Scientist*. Retrieved from http://www.newscientist.com/article/dn17165-six-things-science-has-revealed-about-the-female-orgasm.html

Nuzzo, R. (2008, February 11). Science of the orgasm. *Los Angeles Times*. Retrieved from http://articles.latimes.com/2008/feb/11/health/la-he-orgasm11feb11

Rosen, R. C., Leiblum, S. R. (1987). Current Approaches to the Evaluation of Sexual Desire Disorders. *The Journal of Sex Research*, 23(2), 141-162.

Would Female Orgasms Kill Men? (2007, January 28). *Science 2.0*. Retrieved from http://www.science20.com/science_amp_supermodels/would_female_orgasms_kill_en

YES, MASTER.

Fantasy #1:

A high school couple, Austin and Allison, spend a day at the beach. They swim out past the wave break, and start making out. She wraps her legs around his body, and he begins to finger her. In a trance, she does nothing to stop him as he moves the fabric aside and sticks his dick inside of her. Minutes go by, as they continue to go at it and bob up and down with the waves, wondering if anyone notices that they're doing more than simply kissing.

I don't know about you… But, that's fucking hot! Seriously though? For those of you who have conquered this fantasy, DUH! We all see it. And we all know what's going on beneath the water. Whether it's the ocean, the pool, the lake, the hot tub, or the *Chuck E. Cheeze*'s ball pit, we see it, we're pointing you out to our friends, we're insulting the shit out you, and we're secretly getting insanely jealous for not being in your position.

Why is this hot? Because, a) They're doing it, b) they're doing it in a public place, c) they're doing it in the water, and d) people are watching them. I just hope they were smart enough to leave a hat on the shore for tips. If you're going to give the crowd a show, you might as well make some money off of it.

Fantasy #2:

A lesbian couple, Becca, 28, and Tabs, 36, are on their fourth date. It's obvious that they're going to get busy tonight. Tabs blindfolds her lover with a satin scarf, ties her hands to the head of the bed with a belt, and begins to go down on her partner. As Becca comes close to climaxing, she feels Tab's hand tightening around her throat. The arousal she receives from the pressure around her neck makes her cum instantaneously.

I don't know about you…but, that's fucking hot! I just painted a mini BDSM scene for you with two naked chicks! Have fun with that!

Why is this hot? Because, a) You have two naked chicks going at it, b) one of them is tied up (bondage), leading to c) the fact that she's given up power and trusts the other one enough to be in charge of the sex act (discipline), d) one of the girls is getting off from pain (sadism), and e) the other is getting turned on from providing pain (masochism) by choking her new woman. I think it's safe to say, that the dominant lesbian in this scene doesn't have much experience with choking her own chicken, but if her girlfriend's getting off, she's obviously proficient in her asphyxiaphilic skills.

Fantasy #3:

A married couple, Dave and Jamie, in their late forties decide to go do something new for their "Date Night". They drop the kids off at their sleepover destinations and head out for dinner in the adjacent county. After nervously nibbling on some appetizers, they decline ordering any more courses and proceed to buy a round of shots. Two hours later they enter the local swinger's club.

I don't know about you… But, that's fucking hot! First of all, these two have been married for-who knows how long? They obviously got a little bored and had enough curiosity and communication with each other to try a new sex adventure together. Congratulations to them for having a healthy relationship!

Why is this hot? Because a) They're jumping out of their twenty-odd year comfort zone and trying something new, b) they're leaving their safe zone and trying a new setting, c) they are acting as voyeurs and open to seeing if watching others is going to activate sexual arousal, d) they may choose to act as exhibitionists and strip down to create their own little porn. If they choose to do so, they better be prepared to have a third or fourth party join in. Hopefully, Dave and Jamie have already had the discussion regarding the gender of the key player in their possible threesome, which brings us to e) THREESOME!!!! Or perhaps f) they're open to a full-blown orgy! Either way, I'm sure Dave is ecstatic… Cause no matter what, he's expecting to get fully blown away.

Fantasy #4:

A forty-year old woman, Nicole, just finished cooking herself dinner. As she is pouring herself a glass of wine, she hears the garage door unlock. She becomes alert, fearful, and yet, is turned on. Wondering if it's the mysterious man that she hired to break into her house and rape her, she awaits the arrival of the intruder.

She hears soft footsteps coming towards her from down the hall. She stands frozen on the kitchen floor, knowing that the knives are within arm's reach; but, chooses to leave herself without protection. Thirsty to know who exists around the corner, she tip toes without a sound to the edge of the kitchen. She lays her hands, chest and head against the corner of the wall and shakily breathes. Realizing her noisily breath is giving her location away, she stops. Her eyes widen as she realizes her panting has halted, but the sound of breathing has not. As she slowly gasps for air through her nostrils, she detects a strange, unknown odor of someone else's breath…

She screams as a hand wraps around the corner of the wall and grabs her by the neck. The next thing she feels is her shirt being ripped off of her. She tries to move, but her hands have already been inexplicably bound. As her pants are removed she realizes she feels something dripping down her leg. The doubts that she had been having since she placed the order three months ago have vanished into thin air. She moans in pleasure as the strange man bends her over the kitchen counter and thrusts himself inside of her; and can't help but notice that this most exhilarating sexual purchase was worth every penny.

I don't know about you... But, that's fucking hot! If she hadn't had paid a man to rape her and was waiting impatiently every night for three months, maybe she wouldn't have acted like all dumb-ass bitches in horror films who walk TOWARDS the predator. But then again, maybe all those dumb-ass bitches weren't dumb at all! Perhaps they all just had rape fantasies! This would make sense considering 62% of women fantasize about rape.

Why is this hot? Because a) Someone just broke into her house, putting her in a stressful situation, which raises her dopamine levels, which gets her mind and body ready to enjoy her "rape", which is a type of seduction "fantasy"; meaning, b) she is making contact with someone and abandoning herself to him. c) Being that she has organized this "rape"; the reality is that she has found a way to allow a dangerous situation to occur in her own safety zone: her kitchen. This shows that even though d) she is acting as if she has no control, in her mind, she knows she does. The added bonus to purchasing someone to help her fulfill one of her sexual fantasies is that when all is said and done, if she chooses to never see him again, she doesn't have to. Cause he's a stranger, and she has no obligation to him... Other than to pay up, of course...

Fantasy #5:
A BDSM master, Master John, walks out onto the stage. He approaches the young sex slave, who is lying down on a table, naked. He stares up at the silent, crowded auditorium, and takes a deep breath. He starts placing 102 needles in the male's body.

Carefully, as if an acupuncture therapist, Master John sticks the needles into the male, from head to toe. The boy doesn't move as the needles are being stuck in his scalp, nipples, testicles and feet. When finished, Master John waits for the music to begin.

As classical harp music fills the auditorium hall, the audience of five hundred people is enraptured by watching Master John pluck the strings as if playing a human harp. Soaked in his own blood, the horizontal man, cringes in pleasure as he continuously gets a high from the rushing endorphins to every pluck; acting somewhat like a tiresome, yet jolly puppy.

I don't know about you… But, that's fucking hot! And cracked-out! But seriously… How many people are getting sexually fired up in this one room? This is a crazed-novel sex scene set up for the audience. Not to mention the sexual connection that is occurring between the two players.

Why is this hot? Because a) there are multiple people who don't even know each other who are sharing a sexual experience by being voyeurs and watching a sex show. b) They're anxiety is raised, which increases sexual pleasure; but, they have no guilt because they are not a part of the "heinous", abnormal act; just watching it from afar. c) The classical music produces a calming effect to numb everyone of the shocking scene. As for the two men on stage, d) the harpist is taking pleasure in putting on a show for everyone. The exhibitionist is obviously very passionate of performing art. e) He also is getting off from being the sadist in this occasion. On the other hand, f) the twink is getting off from being the masochist. He has given up his power to the man who is playing him and feels seduced. In the midst of the seduction, g) he is getting aroused from the danger, but has a safe sense of security at the same time. This is all happening while h) he is being pricked with needles, which makes endorphins rush to the location of each and every pluck. The results in i) him being covered in blood. Hey! Some zombie-lovers get really turned on by that shit! Think of all of the men who get turned on when their fucking their ragged up girl!

Sexual fantasies... We all have them. Whether it's trying a new sex position, joining the three mile high club, or getting suffocated with Saran wrap, they're "fantasies" for a reason. It's because fantasies aren't a part of our normal day lives. But just because they're not a part of our normal lifestyle, doesn't mean they're not normal. And just because we don't do them normally, doesn't mean it's not normal to act them out. Get it?!!? Sexual fantasties are NORMAL! (For the most part...)

A little BDSM here and there-NORMAL! A little voyeuristic approach by introducing a pornographic video to your woman-NORMAL! A threesome? NORMAL! Coprophilia? NOT NORMAL! Unlike dogs, humans are not usually turned on by rolling around in someone else's feces. But that doesn't mean people don't do it!

Speaking of paraphilias, a paraphilia is a sexual problem; not just a sexual attraction. The DSM describes a paraphilia as a sexual fantasy that causes unhealthy distress to either the person who suffers from the paraphilia or the non-consenting person(s) involved in the act. Sure, we like to assign each other with random paraphilias. It's all fun! What you do is find a Latin word and add "philia" to the end of it. Want to make fun of your friend for fucking the eye of a jack-o-lantern as a dare when they were sixteen? Look up "eye-socket of pumpkin" in Latin, and BAM! Your fucko friend is a pompionorbitaphilia! It's much more difficult to be diagnosed with paraphilia in the medical world though. In order for you to be labeled as a paraphiliac, it must be an uncontrollable sexual urge that affects your everyday living.

Sure, we may say that Austin and Allison suffer from aquaphilia, since they like doing out in the water. And we may say that Becca and Tabs are both anginophiliacs because they're getting turned on by the act of choking. We may even go as far as saying that Nicole is a harpaxophiliac because she got wet when someone broke into her house... But the chances that these fetishes/sexual preferences are regular occurrences are slim. Austin and Allison probably get off plenty of times behind the closed doors of one of their bedrooms; Becca and Tabs may use different BDSM techniques; and Nicole... Well, Nicole probably doesn't have the money to hire a rapist on a regular basis; and even if she did, the fear would eventually fade away, which would desensitize the whole sexual fantasy.

No matter how extreme your fantasy may be, fantasies are not reality. It's ok. Everyone's attracted to different things because of whatever odd thing happened to them at the age of seven... Or maybe their olfactory sense is just extra attracted to the smell cleanser used in airport bathrooms. Whatever your rare sexual attraction is, as long as it's healthy and not harming you or anyone else, enjoy! Just try not to get arrested...

As for you closet-BDSM, *Fifty Shades* readers, be smart. There are safety rules for a reason. If you choose to act out one of your radical sex fantasies, such as be the victim of a gang rape, plan it out and do it in a controlled setting. Getting gang raped in real life is not the same as joining a respectable BDSM community. A jailbird is not going to give a shit if you can't breathe cause his dick is in your mouth. So, if you're looking for that extreme BDSM activity, be smart about it. Don't think that just because you looked up instructions online, you're the "Master".

In short, the moral of this chapter is to teach you that everyone has fantasies. As you get older, your fantasies will most likely broaden, cause... Well, like you, things get old. But sexuality ripens!

References:

AllPysch Online. (2011). Paraphilias. Retrieved from http://allpsych.com/disorder/paraphilias/index.html

Berger, V. (2005). Diagnostic and statistical manual of paraphilias. Retrieved from http://www.psychologistanywhereanytime.com/sexual_problems_pyschologist/psychologist_paraphilias_list.htm

Bivona, J. & Critelli, J. (2009). The nature of women's rape fantasies: An analysis of prevalence, frequency, and contents. *Journal of Sex Research*, 46(1), 33-45.

Brock, J. (2008). The influence of stress on dopamine levels. Retrieved from http://serendip.brynmawr.edu/exchange/node/1679

James, E. L. (2011). *Fifty Shades of Grey*. United Kingdom: Vintage Books.

Kanin, E. J. (1982). Female rape fantasies: A victimization study. *Victimology*, 7(1-4), 114-121.

Lingis, A. (2012). Seduction. *The Humanistic Psychologist*, 40(1), 109-114.

Master John. (2012, June 18). Interview by TayloR Puck [Phone conversation]. Fantasy.

Strassberg, D. S. & Lockerd, L. K. (1998). Force in women's sexual fantasies. *Archives of Sexual Behavior*, 27, 403-414.

MIND FUCKING

According to the world of Kama Sutra, men can be described as a hare, a bull, or a horse (stallion). Women are described as deer, mares, or elephants. While the ideal combinations may be predicted as a hare and deer, bull and mare, and horse and elephant, this is not the case. The best combinations are described as follows: horse and deer, horse and mare, and bull and deer. But do not fret little men and large women! Thanks to different sexual positions there are still plenty of ways you can master the art of a good fuck! You just need to learn how to use the power of the mind!

Why is this difficult? Well for one, when you get turned on, the blood leaves your brain and rushes down to your genital area; hence, Robin Williams' famous quote, "God gave men both a penis and a brain, but unfortunately not enough blood supply to run both at the same time." Tantra, Kama Sutra, and other teaching methods like *Sensate Focus*, help people improve sexual pleasure, emotional connection with themselves and each other, as well as unlock the mysteries of ancient erotica. Inclusively, Tantra provides spiritual enlightenment, Kama Sutra provides sexually-enhancing techniques, and *Sensate Focus* provides a more personal, therapeutic route. All in all, these three methods help partners relax, focus on themselves, and focus on their partner. If mutual meditation occurs, they will connect sensually and spiritually, which will lead to sexual enlightenment. HELL YEAH!

Tantra means "expansion through awareness". It is a spiritual pathway for sexual energy to travel throughout the body to achieve higher states of consciousness and bliss. Tantra traditions originated in India, Nepal and China. Tantra sex is known for using **sexual union** to reach the enlightenment.

The word, *Kama*, refers to pleasure, desire or sex. The Indian tradition of Kama Sutra describes sex as a sacred practice. And that, it is! This is why you and your one night stand don't try to look deeply into each other's eyes and give each other sensual face massages. According to Vatsyayana Mallanaga, if you perform Kama Sutra correctly, you will find yourself floating somewhere in an enlightened state; somewhere between Earth and heaven. Just make sure to walk AWAY from the light.

Sensate focus is an exercise that allows couples to concentrate on the intimacy of their relationship. Originally created by Masters and Johnson, these exercises incorporate many Tantric and Kama Sutra-like techniques and are known to reduce sexual stress and promote personal awareness. It is a very effective treatment for sexual dysfunctions revolving around desire, arousal and orgasm.

Sexually spiritual and sensual techniques are great for men because they help teach them how to focus on their partner, rather than their instinctive priority: Their dick. Women benefit from these methods because they are able to learn how to relax. While on the Tantric trail, both sexes will learn how to develop a mutual, sexual respect for each other, as well as dive deep into each other's souls. As a result, they will develop an unbreakable trust within each other, and the sexual experience will help solidify every aspect of their relationship.

One extra bonus that these techniques provide novices with is the opportunity to unlearn bad sexual habits. It is extremely easy to gain either negative, or restricted sexual habits throughout the years. For instance, if you are a selfish lover and your prime goal of your sexual experiences is to get yourself off, these activities will take your attention away from **you** and place it on your partner(s). If you have been single for a long time and are only used to enjoying sex with yourself, these activities will allow your partner to learn how to please you the way you prefer, as well as awaken new sexual desires within you.

Finally, if you do the same routine with your partner(s) and they "act" like they're ideal; by incorporating Tantra, Kama Sutra, and *Sensate Focus* into your life, you will take the time to learn better and new ways to make your loved one tick. When you allow yourself time to discover your worlds of sensuality, you will realize that your senses are constantly changing. Just because you could get your girl off within three minutes or less five years ago doesn't mean those techniques are ideal nowadays. Pretend it's day one, and learn each other all over again. Make it a priority to relearn how to please each other on a regular basis.

If you decide to embark the journey of Tantra, start with yourself. The purpose of experiencing Tantra is to experience the ultimate Truth. In essence, you can't truly undergo a Tantric experience with someone else unless you can do it single-handedly. Give yourself practice time and experience just *being*. Try some yoga! Yoga is extremely well-known for improving sexual fulfillment. Not only is it known to improve sexual, mental and physical health; it helps control premature ejaculation, erectile dysfunction, and female orgasm difficulties! Overall, yoga increases strength, improves breathing, reduces stress, and alleviates performance anxiety; therefore, helps people maintain their attention on sex. This is extra important for extremely busy people. A major sexual dysfunction that occurs with active people is a lack of concentration during sexual activity. So relax, breath and jump into downward doggie-style!

After you have learned how to seduce yourself, it's time to communicate how to do so to your partner, and for them to communicate the same to you. Focus on sensuality, not necessarily sexuality. To begin, book each other ahead of time. And when you are in the midst of diving into the sensual realm, don't feel the need to strip down immediately. Perhaps go out to a romantic dinner (don't drink too much), come home and bath each other. Ladies, offer to shave your man's face before you go out. That clean-cut experience can be exhilarating if done correctly. If not, just break out into vampire role-playing. It'll all be good. Men, allow your women to take the blade to your face. (If you decline, it may hurt her feelings.) If nervous, just give her a dull blade. Then in return, ask if she'd like you to shave any of her areas. (Believe me, you'll do a better job than should could ever do.)

Once you get into the naked mode, make sure you reveal to your partner(s) your appreciation for EVERY naked part of their body. Many people have body image issues, and laying naked in front of their partner(s) with the lights on can stir up some major anxiety-no matter how many times you've seen them naked. Trace away! Make it your goal to find EVERY erogenous zone on their body. You can even play the map game. This is when your partner has to rate the sensitivity of every place you touch, on a scale from minus five to positive five. Spend hours on end touching each other's naked bodies. Light some candles, use oils, and massage away. And don't forget the face! I'm not talking about giving your girl a facial. I'm talking about giving her a long, drawn out face massage. Face massages reduce cortisol, a stress hormone, which will help them relax. Tell them to focus on their breathing. A very dominant act is to take control over your partner's(s') breathing, by instructing them to breath with you. When you breath loudly, they focus on maintaining the synchronized breathing and the excess airflow allows them to connect with you. Take your time during this touchy-feely stage. The longer you spend getting comfortable with each other, the more relaxed you'll be when moving on to the next level.

Make music with your mouth! There are plenty of things you can do with your mouth in the bedroom. You can play the harmonica, by rubbing your lips up and down a penis, you can hum a tune on someone's clitoris, and you can moan a song as you reach orgasm. And then there's the obvious: kissing, licking, blowing, sucking and nibbling every part of your partner's(s') body(ies). Again, spend hours orally exploring your partner(s). Trail your tongue from behind their ears, down the neck, behind the shoulder blades, down the spine, over the ass, into the taint, around their genitals, down their thighs, in the back of their knees, circle the ankles, and in between their toes. Finally, when your mouths are tired from doing everything EXCEPT talking, you may move on to the genital stimulation.

Kama Sutra is most known for its sexual positions; although most of them are named after an animal, i.e., "Congress of a Crow", or in the numerical sense, "69". So whether you're trying to embrace the monkey, tame the lion, charm the snake, or batter two rams, all you really need is a floor, a wall, perhaps some pillows, and a bed. An ottoman is always a nice addition to your sexplay. (Always keep that in mind when furniture shopping.) As for swinging sex chairs and monkey bars, these expensive accessories are fun; but, not necessary for you to master the art of fucking with your minds.

Then again… You can get crazy with some of those acrobatic positions!!! I've said it before and I'll say it again… The *Sarah Marshall* bridge IS possible! And if you're bodies are proportionate and strong, I would suggest trying the following:

The banqueting table: The man gets in crab mode, but lifts his butt into the air, so that his back is flat and parallel to the floor. The woman then lies, stomach down, on top of him. She places her hands on the floor to prop her front up and lets her feet rest along side of his ears. Once the penis is in place, they rock back and forth to simulate sexual satisfaction.

Autumm dog: Both partners get in downward-facing dog and back up against each other so their asses are touching. As they lean on their hands or shoulders, they arch their backs while pushing their butts high in the air in order to provide extra closeness for their genital regions.

Barrow position: This one's simply the wheel-barrow position where the taker has their hands up against the wall, and their legs in the air.

Teasing the jade stem: The man is bent over with his hands up against the wall. His partner is lying on top of his back with their face in his ass. Would you like ranch or balsamic vinaigrette with that?

During this whole sexual extravaganza, orgasms will hopefully be manifesting. And although it should not be your main goal, there are different types that may result from your Tantric experience. The cosmorgasm affects the universe. It's when you unleash the sexual energy through the top of your head, your crown chakra, and release it into the atmosphere above. The mega-orgasm resembles the *Energizer* bunny. "It keeps going, and going..." The clearing orgasm brings out powerful emotions. This one can result in painful screams and tears. Don't be afraid if you cause someone to sexually express themselves in this way. Take pride in the fact that you provided them with the opportunity to free their mind, body and soul. The Tantric orgasm provides undulating, wave-like orgasms. These are much more fun than orgasming in wave pool, considering there is a lot less urine involved. And finally, an orgasm created by sexpert, Ava Cadall: the stock market orgasm! This has seven peaks and seven dips, representing the unpredictable highs and lows, but hopefully profitable outcome. Just make sure to you and your partner(s) finish before Obama gets re-elected. (I obviously wrote that last sentence *before* the last election. Now that all is written and done- Go Obama!)

References:

Apatow, J., Robertson, S., & Rothman, R. (Producers), & Stoller, N. (Director). (April 18, 2008). *Forgetting Sarah Marshall* [Motion picture]. United States: Apatow Productions.

Bailey, N. (2005). *Pure Kama Sutra.* London: Duncan Baird Publishers.

Brotto, L.A., Mehak, L. & Kit, C. (2009). Yoga and sexual functioning: A review. *Journal of Sex & Marital Therapy*, 35, 378-390.

Dempsey, B. (n.d.) Kama Sutra and Tantra. Retrieved from http://www.netplaces.com/Tantric-sex/history-of-Tantric-sex/kama-sutra-and-Tantra.htm

DiscoveryHealth.com. (2012). Sensate focus. Retrieved from http://health.howstuffworks.com/sexual-health/sexuality/sensate-focus-dictionary.htm

DK Publishing. (2008). *Kama Sutra 365.* London: *Author.*

Hooper, A. (2000). *Guide to the Kama Sutra.* London: DK Publishing.

Kuriansky, J. (2004). *Tantric Sex.* New York: Penguin Group.

Stanford School of Medicine. (2012). Sensate focus. Retrieved from http://womenshealth.stanford.edu/fsm/sensate_focus.html

The Wall Street Journal. (2012). Massage proves to have medical benefits. *Fox News.* Retrieved from http://www.foxnews.com/health/2012/03/14/massage-proves-to-have-medical-benefits/

Sexualization

This circle of sexuality revolves around power over others. Its major components include: Flirting, media messages, seduction, withholding sex, sexual harassment, incest, and rape.

THE CAT

Biologists say that our most basic, evolutionary goal in life is to reproduce. How does one reproduce? Well, we are not amoebas, flowers nor sponges. We reproduce via fucking! How lucky are we?

The evolution of social hierarchy *makes* us have sex. We kind of *have to*, in the name of Science. But, the real reason why we are lucky that we have to sexually reproduce is because we, as humans, actually have the capacity to enjoy the art of love making.

Lions have spines on their dicks. So, when the male pulls out, the "stimulation" of the spines raking across the vagina causes ovulation. Wow! That sounds pleasurable! Before porcupines go at it, the male waddles over to his Lady, stands on his hind legs ~6 feet away, and uses her as a target for his stream of piss. Speaking of golden showers, a male giraffe nudges the bum of the female until she pees. Then, he drinks her pee in order to detect if she's ovulating. A drone gets to fuck a virgin queen! This sounds awesome! What's not so awesome is that the honey bee's testicles explode off of him when he's done. Talk about bustin' a nut! And that's not even the worst of a bug's life... We all know of the untimely death that occurs with the praying mantis. I guess the question is, would you rather die a virgin, or get your head ripped off right after you cum?

Like us humans, some animals have sex for recreational purposes, because they ACTUALLY get pleasure from the act. We know dolphins do it for sexual gratification, because we've actually witnessed them gang-raping each other (and you thought they were such perfect, little creatures), and bonobos... Well, they just fuck each other every chance they get. So since we share 98.7% of our DNA with these little monkeys, next time you're monkeying around with your significant other, or going ape-shit in the bedroom, you're not too far off... Evolutionarily...

Everyone in the animal kingdom has sex in common; mammals especially. Sex affects the same primitive parts of the brain. But for humans, sex has evolved into a much more complex concept than a simple biological phenomenon. We do it for a majority of reasons; not just to procreate or enjoy a little sexual pleasure. Meston and Buss (2007) did a study to find out reasons why humans have sex. They found at least 237 reasons. Did you get that?!?!? There are AT LEAST 237 reasons why people have sex! These reasons/excuses included, "I wanted to make my partner feel better about themselves", "I wanted to say 'goodnight'", "I got turned on by the conversation", "I wanted to relate at a more 'deeper' level", "I wanted to get a raise" and "I was drunk". Participants were able to make up ANY excuse to have sex... And you wonder why everything has to involve sex. Well, it's because we live in a sex-driven world!

Sex is powerful! It is a form of stress reduction. It gives us pleasure and physical desirability. It is a stimulating experience. It can provide us with resources, or give us social status. It can be a form of revenge. It gets us high. It gives people the feeling of love and commitment. It is a form of expression. Sadly enough, it can boost self-esteem. So since we have found all of these OTHER reasons why we should have sex other than to have babies, humankind has evolved to accomplish the goal of sexually 'getting off' with or without a mating partner. Examples include masturbation, sex with the same sex, friends with benefits, rape, and teledildonics. For those of you who don't know, teledildonics are computer regulated devices that get people off. They work extremely well for long-distance relationships that have sex via computer, as well as handicapped people, i.e. quadriplegics. Yes, even paralyzed people need ways to get off. Just because they can't use the majority of their bodies doesn't mean they can't use ANY of it. It's not like they're asexual… They, too, still have a need for sex. Pretty cool, huh?

Parents usually do their best to explain to their children when talking about the 'birds and the bees' that sex is "special". To their daughters, especially… And yes, sex is "special", but it is also "powerful". The power of the pussy, or what I like to call it, the power of "the cat", can be one of the most powerful tools a human can learn to use. But like all power, there are positive AND negative ways for you to use it.

We all have the ability to have sex. And whether you choose to do it with yourself or someone else, you should make sure you're not abusing that power. One obvious example of negatively using sex is prostitution. Yes, there are pros when it comes to prostitution; but culturally, it is known to be more harmful than helpful. A less obvious example of using sex in a negative light is masturbating purely for the sole purpose of 'getting off'. Synonyms that describe this act are flogging the monkey, busting a load, choking the chicken, flicking the bean, flitting the clit, gagging the clam, beating around the bush, poaching the salmon, arm-wrestling the purple-headed stormtrooper, banging the bishop, pummeling the one-eyed trouser snake, punching the midget, cranking the shank, slammin' the salami, jerkin' the joystick, whacking off, and yanking Yoda. Talk about negative association! When was the last time you made love to your genitals? Yes, when people are masturbating, they're usually rushing in hopes that their parents/spouse doesn't come home; but again, this "viscous" rushed habit will only bring about a future sexual dysfunction. Learn to make love to your genitals, instead of simply aiming for the climatic event. Seriously… I know it sounds weird, but try masturbating in a more loving manner. Learn to fully appreciate stimulation that you're giving to yourself. Then, when you're becoming intimate with someone else, you'll have a more affectionate and sweet sexual aura about you, instead of rushing right through it.

It is important for you to learn the value of sex before you distribute your body as a sexual tool to assist others. Whatever their excuse is, your body is a temple and it's yours. Not theirs. So, it's up to you on who you share it with. You have your own sex-opoly, which means that you control who you share the power with.

For all of you virgins out there; if you are holding off on having sex for religious, moral, or self purposes, so be it! Do not give in to sexual temptations until you are ready. In your case, withholding sex is appropriate and healthy.

On the other hand, if you're already in an intimate monogamous, sexual relationship with someone else, withholding sex is **not** a well-played move. It's like not giving your dog food anymore, in hopes that it learns new tricks. Whatever message you are trying to get across to your partner by withholding sex, it's probably not going to work. Withholding sex from your partner is a very dangerous tactic because it creates an uneven balance between partners, changing the equality of the relationship. Yes, it is assumed that within every 'give and take', there is a shift in power; but, through every negotiation or "compromise" one will always inequitably gain dominance over the other, resulting in variance of balance. If one exerts their power continuously, resentment will grow due to the uneven balance. In order to correct the problem, it will take a huge effort from both people to recalibrate the scale. The ultimate question will be, "Do both partners have the energy to make it work?"

As for gay men… Don't be offended by the term, "Pussy Power". Just because you hear about the power of the pussy all of the time, doesn't mean you don't have the power because you lack the cat! I mean if we're going to compare apples to oranges here, you win! Cause you have a trunk! And an elephant is a much

larger and more powerful animal than a cat. Unless it's a lion...
And there's thirty of them. That's really the only way a lion can take
an elephant down, according to *Youtube*. Why can't they all just
get along and hang out with *Randall* and his honey badgers under
the Marula tree? They can all just get high and not give a shit.

References:

Czg123. "Honey Badger Narrates: The Intoxicating Marula Trees of South Africa (Original Narration by Randall)." Online video clip. *YouTube.* YouTube, 28, June 2011. Web. 11, Oct. 2012.

Gibbons, A. (2012, June 13). Bonobos join chimps as closest human relatives. *Science NOW.* Retrieved from http://news.sciencemag.org/sciencenow/2012/06/bonobo-genome-sequenced.html

Meston, C. M. & Buss, D. M. (2007). Why humans have sex. *Archives of Sexual Behavior, 36,* 477-507.

Nixon, R. (2009). Do animals enjoy sex? *Live Science.* Retrieved from http://www.livescience.com/9631-animals-enjoy-sex.html

Santer, R. (2007, April 30). 30 strangest animal mating habits. Retrieved from http://www.neatorama.com/2007/04/30/30-strangest-animal-mating-habits/

Scott, E.M., Mann, J., Watson, J. J., Sargaent, B. L. & Connor, R. C. (2005). Aggression in bottlenose dolphins: Evidence for sexual coercion male-male competition, andfemaletolerance through analysis of tooth-rake marks and behaviour. *Behaviour, 142,* 21-44.

Simcha. (2009, February 18). 10 shockingly weird animal sex habits. Retrieved from http://www.thefrisky.com/2009-02-18/10-reasons-you-dont-want-him-to-f-you-like-an-animal/

WHAT'S YOUR THEME SONG?

Whenever I walk into a room, I imagine the intro to Duffy's "Mercy" playing in the background while I stroll in. Oh! Did I fail to mention that everyone in the room is holding hand-held, battery-operated fans and pointing them in my direction? That way, my appearance will resemble a *Pantene Pro-V* commercial every time I enter a room.

But in all seriousness, do you ever feel as though you're playing the wrong part in the wrong movie? We all want to be the protagonist that stars in a romantic comedy filled with action and hot sex scenes. And a killer music soundtrack? BONUS! Unfortunately, sometimes the role we play in real life doesn't pan out the way we'd prefer. But that's ok, because every passing minute is another chance to turn it all around!

Ask yourself this: What percentage of *your* movie is original? And what percentage is copied? This can be a sad reality check for some of you. You'd like to think that the role you play in life is truly unique, and the character performance is solely copyrighted by you. I mean, it's your thoughts, your choices, and your actions that lead you to the next scene, right? But truthfully, how much influence do *you* have on *yourself*?

In life, there are innate behaviors and there are learned behaviors. Because most humans have been blessed with five senses, they are able to exponentially obtain knowledge as they age. Yes, when we are born, we are not taught how to breathe. We innately do the act because our parasympathetic system takes the controls over to ensure our survival. But, the things we consciously do are affected by our learned knowledge, content that we've gained from observing. We make decisions based on things that we have learned thus far.

Where do we learn these things from? Well, we have our parents, siblings, friends, teachers and role models; but this day in age, what may be even more influential is the powerful mass media. You are constantly exposed to movies, television, songs, the internet, books, magazines, and advertising campaigns. And these messages that the mass media relays are attractive to you because they are fresh new voices, new ideas. They stimulate your brain because they are usually bringing things to your attention that you aren't used to on a regular basis, i.e. news, fashion, art, and culture. Late at night your mom may have sung you lullabies when you were a child, but did she break out in Lady Gaga clothes and lyrics? (Hopefully not, cause I can only assume that that experience would be a tad scary for a four year old... Then again... I guess that depends on their sexual orientation...)

Why are these media messages so powerful? Because the new information catches your attention! They're out of the ordinary; therefore, you start acting like Dory when she came in contact with the angler fish. Not only are you attracted to the messages, but if you're under the age of thirty, your views on gender roles, sexual attitudes and sexual behaviors are in the midst of being molded; therefore, depending on what you pick up can be a scary situation.

When you're an adolescent, you have time to be "deep" and "find yourself". (A side note: If you're out of college, don't ever tell your date that you are one of the two. Just go get a fucking job.) So, you sit in your room after a fresh break-up, listen to music, and you find a song that is appealing to your ear. You listen to it again, and then start focusing on the lyrics. You hear, "Yeah, I was dreaming for so long… I wish I knew then, what I know now… Falling from cloud nine…"and you begin to relate to the song. "Oh my God! This is *SO* me!" The emotional attachment that grows between you and the song throws the mere thought out the window that these are the most **wide**-ranging lyrics, and could be associated with *anyone* who was just released from a relationship. That does not cross your mind though, because now… You're "Wide Awake".

You play this song over and over and over again. Every time, you reminisce about your former significant other and recognize the fact that you are no longer "on the concrete". You grow stronger with every play of the tune, and what you don't realize is that twenty years later, when you're driving your kids to school and this "oldie" comes on the radio, your thoughts are going to circle right back to this point in your life. You'll remember that relationship as if it were yesterday and the song will still give you chills and bring tears to your eyes.

Why does this happen? Because of good ol' dopamine, of course! Dopamine is a chemical that is released from the brain during eating, sexual encounters or other rewarding experiences, such as listening to pleasurable music. This chemical is associated with attraction, seeking pleasure, and reward. High levels of dopamine in the brain produce steady motivation and extremely focused attention. So, it doesn't help that at your age you're critically analyzing every mass media message coming your way. Your mom may have to repeatedly tell you to do your laundry three times a week for eleven years of your life, but Wiz Khalifa and Snoop Dogg don't have to tell you twice about how cool 501 jeans are. Once you hear them singing about how good partying is when you're wearing those 501s, you become obsessed. You want those damn jeans! And your mom, of course buys them for you, in hopes that you'll respond by washing them on a regular basis.

If you wonder how affected you are by mass media, the answer is: A lot more than your grandparents were. If the messages are readily available on television, billboards, your cells phone, the internet, etc., it's inevitable: You're going to learn from them. This is why every approaching generation gets smarter. Lazier, but smarter. Information is constantly available and people are gaining larger quantities of content knowledge. Perfect social media example: *Facebook*. A study revealed that students who check *Facebook* every fifteen minutes during their study period achieve lower grades in school. That's because you find your friends' break-up statuses more interesting than the American Revolution. Duh. I would too! Think about it: You can scroll down a *Facebook* page once, memorize all of status updates, news reports and downloaded apps; yet, you have to reread a page in your history text over and over again. Sounds to me like we have to rethink America's education system! Because at this point in time, Mark Zuckerberg seems to have better teaching strategies than the United States' Department of Education!

Albert Bandura is the psychologist who came up with the social learning theory. This theory states that people learn from observing, imitating and modeling each other. The model bridges the gap between other behaviorist theories and cognitive theories because it encompasses attention, memory and motivation. According to Bandura's theory, the four conditions needed in order to learn a behavior are: 1) Attention, 2) retention, 3) reproduction, and 4) motivation. We give our attention to something or someone, we retain the information, we reproduce the same image, and we are motivated to do it ourselves.

Let's discuss porn, shall we? I can almost positively assure you that the sex that you are having, or will have in your life will be more wild than your great-great-grandparents' sex. Why? Because we're lucky enough to have porn. Porn is awesome! Most of what you know about sex is from pornography. What exactly is pornography? Well, according to Supreme Court Justice Potter Stewart, *you'll know it when you see it*. This shit cracks me up. We have laws on porn; but yet, we can't *define* porn. Well, aside from that ass-backwards fact, we are exposed to many sexual things. Whether it's porn, a love scene in a movie, *The Bachelor/ Bachelorette*, or the front cover of a magazine, we see sexual behaviors and like Bandura's Social Learning Theory, we learn from them.

A boy watches his first porn at the age of thirteen. He sees where to put his hands, where to put his tongue and where to put his dick in order to make her cum. He has given his attention to the film, retained the information, and will reproduce the image when he finds a willing mate. Why? Because he's motivated for the reward: The squirt! This is fine, because when he does have his first sexual experience with a girl he'll at least have a *slight* clue on what he's doing. Unfortunately, his sexual mentality is somewhat warped. He's lost somewhere between the sexual realms of reality vs. fantasy.

First of all, most first sexual experiences take place in a darkened private area; not in a lit up room with a silky couch and the pizza delivery boy acting as a voyeur. Second, people usually don't look as hot as they do in porns (there is no make-up artist working on either of you before the scene), especially when you start sweating your ass off because the pumping is getting out of control. In a porn, the usual formula for an average sex scene is "kiss-kiss-suck-suck-rim-fuck-change positions-fuck-cum-cum" (Scuglia, 2004). Let me just tell ya: In order to get that double cum shot; well let's just say it's not that easy. The average porn scene can take up to eight hours to film. You'll be lucky if your sex scene takes up to one hour. And you can't cut out scenes. If a queef or fart pops out, there's no way to erase it. Also, unless you're doing it Californian style with a mirror on the ceiling, there are no aerial views. You only see the beauty of what's in front of your own two eyes. Sure, you can flip each other around, bend your neck and brighten or dim the lights; but, you're limited when watching your own sex scene. Finally, only six percent of women actually squirt. So, when your woman fails to do so, don't blame yourself. Some of it's urine anyway… You're better off without the pissy cum shot. Ultimately, you can try to act like a porn star, but let's face it: You're not.

Alas! There is good news! Most porn stars are just meeting each other for the first time before these "struggling actors" have a good fuck. You, on the other hand, are hopefully experiencing sex with someone who you know fairly well; possibly with someone you love! This will add to your experience immensely. And even though you may not look like Ron Jeremy in the act, you still have potential for a perfect fuck!

Back to mass media-it's not going anywhere. And like a pre-aroused dick, it's only going to get bigger. As stated earlier, the impact of these messages can be scary. There are plenty of examples of media messages gone bad: Super models producing body image issues, rappers suggesting drug usage, television shows and networks glorifying teenage pregnancies (fucking ridiculous). What happens is sometimes these messages are delivered to people like you and you are mature enough to be influenced by them, but not mature enough to deal with the consequences of them.

An easy example is experimenting with drugs, alcohol and sex. Plain and simple: All three things can be extremely dangerous if certain precautions aren't taken. Media messages regarding these three topics are usually viewed in a positive light, and the negative consequences that can arise from negligence may not be recognized by the viewer. So, if you do try them out for size, please be careful and do your best to make smart decisions.

Another example is prom. Media messages can destroy this special evening! The concept of the "perfect evening" is depicted as the path to personal fulfillment and happiness. This is maintained by magazine and television shows every year come spring. The student will paint this picture in their head of the perfect evening, and no matter how much fun everyone's having, if the actual event doesn't resemble their preplanned vision, they can go crazy and automatically feel as though everything's ruined. I don't want to stereotype girls here, but it's not sexist if it's true. It's just true. It's not rare for a girl to become a raging psycho bitch when it comes to her prom night. As a result, her date gets pissed off because they realize they're not going to attain the notorious label as the "devirginizer". At least not this weekend.

A more extreme example of when mass media can really fuck someone up is when they become obsessed with a message. A girl is in a six month relationship with her boyfriend. She breaks up with him out of the blue. While he's in tears begging her for an explanation of why she is breaking his heart, she responds with, "You're just not my Edward."

What the fuck?

Well, it's probably best that this girl remains by herself for a while; considering she's not only in search of a "perfect" boyfriend, but a "fictional" boyfriend for that matter.

What youngsters don't understand is that romance portrayed in media has no relevance when it comes to "real life". You may be searching for the perfect person in your life, and that's ok! But always remember, the only person who you have control over is yourself. So when it comes to love, you're never going to have a sure thing. Unless you buy a puppy. Puppies are filled with unconditional love.

Whether you're actively seeking media messages or accumulating them passively, you must learn how to make your own choices that aren't solely based on a promoter's business. So, as you continue to be affected by the world around you, be aware as you negotiate your identity. Do your best to be the most influenced by **you**, and not others. Remember, this is your story. You are the creator, writer, producer, director and main character. So, focus on the one thing you can control-yourself; and make your movie your favorite movie.

References:

Bandura, A. (1977). *Social Learning Theory*. New York: General Learning Press.

Bleakley, A., Hennessy, M., & Fishbein, M. (2011). A model of adolescents' seeking of sexual content in their media choices. *Journal of Sex Research*, 48(4), 309-315.

Committee on Communications, American Academy of Pediatrics. (1995). Sexuality, contraception and the media. *Pediatrics*, 95, 298-300.

Delvin, D. (2011) Female ejaculation. Retrieved from http://www.netdoctor.co.uk/sexandrelationships/female_ejaculation.htm

FML. (2009). Retrieved from www.fmylife.com/love/9321

Galician, M.L. & Merskin, D.L. (2007). *Critical thinking about sex, love, and romance in the mass media*. Mahwah, NJ: Lawrence Erlbaum Associates.

Lowry, D.T. & Towles, D.E. (1989). Prime time TV portrayals of sex, contraception, and venereal diseases. *Journalism Q*, 66, 347-352.

Lowry, D.T. & Towles, D.E. (1989). Soap opera portrayals of sex, contraception, and sexually transmitted diseases. *J Commun*, 66, 76-83.

Perry, K., McKee, B., Gottwald, L., Martin, M., Walter, H. (22, May 2012). Wide Awake [Recorded by Katy Perry]. On *Teenage Dream: The Complete Confection* [CD]. Los Angeles, CA: Dr. Luke-Cirkut.

Scuglia, B. (2004). Sex pigs: Why porn is like sausage, or the truth is that-behind the scenes-porn is not very sexy. *Journal of Homosexuality*, 47(3/4), 185-188.

Youth Research. (2011, August 15). Research confirms social media's impact on adolescent development. *Evansville Courier & Press*. Retrieved from http://www.courierpress.com/news/2011/aug/15/research-confirms-social-medias-impact-on/

Walters, G. (Producer), & Stanton, A. (Director). (May 30, 2003). *Finding Nemo* [Motion picture]. United States: Pixar Animation Studios.

Zlatunich, N. (2009). Prom dreams and prom reality: Girls negotiating "perfection" at the high school prom. *Sociological Inquiry*, 79(3), 351-375.

SUCK MY DICK! IT'S A GEM!

> Are you from Ireland? Because my dick is Dublin!
> 'Sex' is not the answer. Sex is a question. 'Yes'
>   is the answer.
> Does this napkin smell like chloroform to you?
> Is there a mirror in your pocket? Cause I can see
>   myself in your pants!
> Do you believe in love at first sight? Or should I
>   walk by again?
> Are you from Tennessee? Cause you're the only ten
>   I see around here!
> Can I buy you a drink? Or do you just want my
>   money?
> Let's go back to my place and do things I'll tell
>   everyone we did anyway.
> If I could rearrange the alphabet, I'd put you 'U' and
>   'I' together.
> Are you a fan of fancy jewels? Suck my dick!
>   It's a gem!

Flirtation is fucking awesome. Everyone does it! And even though it's usually associated with sexual intentions; that is very often NOT the case. Matthew Abrahams defined flirting as "messages and behaviors perceived by a recipient as purposefully attempting to gain his or her attention and stimulate his or her interest in the sender, while simultaneously being perceived as intentionally revealing an affiliative desire". Although a loving approach, people use flirtation as a tactic to determine any sort of interpersonal relations. You can deduce a lot about another person by the way they react to your flirtation. Since flirtation is extremely informing, AND FUN-for that matter, people do it for several reasons. David Henningsen determined six types of motivations for flirtatious behaviors; they are as follows: 1) Instrumental, 2) Self-esteem, 3) exploring, 4) relational, 5) fun, & 6) sexual. These six motivations review the different reasons why one might exhibit flirtatious behavior.

Instrumental:

Instrumental motivation describes flirting that is exhibited because the flirter is trying to get something out of the flirtee. As discussed before, many people believe that flirtatious behavior is only exuded between romantic partners. When referring to instrumental motivation, clear-cut examples elucidate that flirting can occur between the most unromantic of all people. A common example is between a teacher and a student. Yes, it is true that teachers flirt with students and vice versa. Disagree? Examples of flirting involve the following: Eye contact, a smile, laughter, extra attention… If a teacher feels that their extra attention is going to make a student work harder, they're going to focus on that student! Instrumental flirtation does not always indicate that physical sexual advances are going to occur. The flirter is simply trying to get something completely unsexual from the flirtee. And does it work?!? Yes.

A NOT so perfect example of this is Miss Debra Lafave. I mean, she was *definitely* trying to get something out of her student, but it was not extra participation during class time. It was more like she was helping him bone up on his studies!

Sexualization

A perfect example of an instrumental motivated flirtatious act would be a female bartender with one of her regulars. She hands the man the bill. "Here's the tab," she announces.

"Can I give you 'just the tip'?" he asks jokingly.

The bartender slyly smiles and answers, "No. I just want your money, Honey." Then, she finishes the conversation off with a wink.

He sighs as he shakes his head with a smile and lays down a one-hundred dollar bill.

Self-Esteem:
One of the main reasons why all genders flirt is to improve their self-esteem. If one opens up the possibility to be flirted back with, and they receive the coquettish retaliation they will be flattered! This is just an occupational speculation, but a girl who works at *Hooters* probably has a higher self-esteem than someone who works at *Chotchkies*. Why? Because she has chosen a career where she is constantly flirted with by hundreds or even thousands of men! Imagine putting yourself in a position where you are receiving hundreds or thousands of compliments a week. You're self-esteem is bound to soar! Now, if someone doesn't think so highly of themselves, they will avoid instigating the flirtatious banter; but, they might give someone "the eye", in hopes to let them know that they are invited to come over and let bidding begin. It's safe to say, that people who instigate flirtatious behavior on a regular basis have a higher self-esteem than others; that, or rejection just doesn't bum them out as much.

Whoa, whoa, whoa… What is 'the eye'?, you may be thinking. "The eye" is the most discreet mode of flirtation, and is commonly used by people with shy personalities. If someone is giving you "the eye" it means that they have caught your gaze, not once, not twice, but three times! By the third hit, the eye contact *should* be elongated into a gaze, followed by a smile. If you receive "the eye" from someone, but the third time is not a charm-get a clue! For instance, instead of a gaze followed by a smile, if the person notices that you caught their eye and they quickly look away *as if* the connection never happened, avoid this person at all costs and STOP LOOKING AT THEM! It is at this point that *they* are looking at their friends and saying, "This creep keeps staring at me!"

The only thing worse than running into a Jersey Shore Guido, is running into a Jersey Shore Guido who moonlights as a police officer. Whether these guys are flashing their badges at the bars or flaunting their sweet, new Affliction t-shirts, these douchebag cops are seeking validation to boost their self-esteem from the women they show their prized possession to. Chances are that even if the girl being shown the respected property thinks the guy is a tool, she'll still show some sign of enthusiastic captivation; especially, if she's had a few and plans on driving home. There are certainly more intelligent things she can do than make an enemy out of a po-po.

Exploring:
Are they interested in the bait? Someone who uses flirtation as an exploration device is one who is trying to determine how interested another person might be. The flirter plans on tossing a line out and is hoping for a nibble; not necessarily a bite. For instance, a woman may be toying with the idea of becoming a little informal with a formal co-worker. If she's curious to find out if there's a possibility, she may flirt with them to see what their response is. If she receives any reciprocation, she can then, reassess the situation and find out if she wants to partake in the risky business and let things to continue in that direction.

An online dating introduction is usually instigated by exploration motivation. A smart person will simply send the word, "Hi," to the user that they're interested in. The word, "hi," or any other short note of interest is a great way to let someone know that you're interested, because it doesn't waste your time. The reality is that half of the people you write to on an online dating website don't even look at your first message. If contacted by you, the first thing they're going to do is blow up your profile picture to see if they're physically attracted to you, followed by reading your profile to see if you cover the majority of their 'checklist'. THEN, and only then, will they simply reply with a "hi" back. And what that means is, "Hey! I'm bored out of my mind and you're hot with some potential. How do you like your eggs cooked?"

Relational:
When someone is in a relationship and they are interested in taking it to the next level, their flirting is usually motivated by relational purposes. For instance, if you have a fuck buddy and would like to "up" your relationship to the next level, you may flirt with more emotion, by using the phrase, "Honey, would you make me a snack?"; rather than, "Make me a sandwich, Bitch!" If your catercousin graciously accepts your more intimate terms without hesitation, it may be a sign that they too, are willing to intensify the relationship.

Another example would be a girlfriend giving her boyfriend a sweet, unexpected gift for no reason. He excitedly opens it up, only to have a flacid reaction when he pulls the cock ring out of the box. He stares at her expecting an explanation. She responds in a plucky voice, "It's been over three years. I thought it was time I bought you a ring…"

Fun:
Some people flirt, purely because they enjoy the act, itself. Usually people who flirt for fun are labeled as "a tease". Frequent flirters, who actually get enjoyment out of the promiscuous act, can consider flirting an actual hobby! And if that is the case, and they spend their spare time mastering the system, they are usually VERY good at what they do. As they become more dominant in the flirting scene, they may up the ante each time to make it a competition with themselves.

For instance, an average-looking girl sees a good-looking

guy who resembles Ryan Gosling, a notoriously *gorgeous-looking* actor, at a bar. She approaches him. "Ryan!" She says. He slants his eyebrows with a confused look on his face. "Ryan Gosling, right?" she asks.

He laughs at her sly way of hitting on him. "Yes," he says. "And you are?"

"Lauren," she responds. The rest of the night, Lauren constantly refers to the man by the name of Ryan, knowing that every time she does, it boosts his self-esteem; which in turn makes him want to be around her more and more. By the end of the night, "Ryan" has asked Lauren for her number. *That was fun! Let's see who's next*, Lauren thinks as she walks away from "Ryan" without a care in the world if he even calls her the next day.

Sexual:
Finally, flirtation that is derived from sexual motivation is usually obvious and unambiguous. When one is hoping for a sexual interaction, their flirtation is most likely going to come off as assertive and promiscuous. But then again, depending on one's personality, they may be looking for a purely physical outcome, but be very bad at indicating that through flirtation. Although all of the flirting motivations may result in a sexual encounter, the flirter who is purely focused on the sexual intent has one thing on their mind.

An easy example of blunt, sexual motivational flirtation is a man slapping a woman's ass. Depending on the location and context of the flirtation, he may receive a slap in return, across the face. On the other hand, if it's occurring at a strip club it will be a bit more acceptable. A simple, "How much?" with a sexy eye lift will let a woman know she's wanted. If she doesn't answer, he may take the next step, whip out his credit card and swipe it through her ass as she's giving his co-worker a lap dance. Depending on how high class the strip joint is, he'll either end up tossin' dollars at her and making it rain, or he'll chuck quarters her way for more of a hailing effect.

The six flirting motivations have been clearly demarcated above. Unfortunately, when trying to decipher why one is flirting with you, it is not as easy as using the process of elimination to determine the basis of motivation. The majority of the time, people flirt for several, if not all motivational reasons. This mixture of motives can sometimes lead to a world of confusion.

Not only is the motivational factor hard to translate, but the context of the flirting can also be difficult to read. Different people have different personalities. Their approach is different, their intellect is different, their sense of humor is different, and most importantly, their perspective is different. Someone who is flirting sarcastically is going to come off as one of the following ways: 1) Absolutely hilarious, 2) an absolute asshole, 3) absolutely full of themselves, or 4) absolutely insecure. That's fucked up, isn't it?!?!! You'd think that if you were sarcastically flirting with someone, you'd come off as witty and fun. But, that's not always the case, unfortunately.

Not only is it hard to decipher the truth behind flirting with someone you do or do not know well, it's difficult to understand the opposite sex's point of view. You see, men perceive flirting completely differently than women. The majority of the times, men see the act of flirtation as sexually driven. They don't realize that women's playful interactions are mostly performed for fun! Here's something COMPLETELY INTERESTING: Women are more attracted to men who flirt for sexual purposes, rather than for fun. And here's another thing: Women who flirt for "friendly reasons" think that the men who are flirting back are flirting back for "friendly reasons". *What the FUCK! I JUST WANT TO GET LAID!*

If you do find yourself in the clueless world of mixed messages, here are some simple rules you should abide by: 1) If someone is flirting with you, that *doesn't* mean that they automatically want to sleep with you. 2) A man assumes that if a woman is flirting with him, she wants to suck his dick. (Women, take note! If you are a flirtatious bitch, most men will become more sexually aggressive, the more you flirt. Be careful!) 3) Flirtation is a form of communication that can easily be misunderstood. The types of problems that can occur between a flirtatious exchange are miscommunication, attempted communication and misinterpretation. Miscommunication is when the message received on the flirtee's end is different than the message that was intended by the flirter. Attempted communication is when the message that is being sent by the flirter is not received by the flirtee. Finally, misinterpretation is when an unintended form of communication is read incorrectly by another person; for instance, a girl has dust in her eye and keeps winking at her boss. In turn he thinks she is hitting on him. All three of these communication problems can make flirtation come off as a very tedious game.

If you're not getting a clear message, and your exploring and relational motivation has hit the threshold, it's time to be more blunt: Ask your flirter/flirtee out on a date! If you don't, the game may stop. People terminate their flirtatious behavior because of exhaustion all of the time! If they feel as though they have exerted enough energy and aren't getting what they want out of flirting with you, all they have to do is look in a different direction to find a different target. For those of you men out there who are not so good at closing the deal, you'd better go buy *How to Get Laid in Less Than Three Dates*. That way you're flirtation is bound to be rewarded with some pussy!

References:

Abrahams, M.F. (1994). Perceiving flirtatious communication: An exploration of the perceptual dimensions underlying judgments of flirtatiousness. *Journal of Sex Research*, 31, 282-292.

Funny2.com. (2012). Pickup Lines #2. Retrieved from http://funny2.com/pickupb.htm

Hecht, M.L., Devito, J.A.& Guerrero, L.K. (1999). Perspectives on nonverbal communication: Codes, functions, and contexts.

Henningsen, D.D. (2004). Flirting with meaning: An examination of miscommunication in flirting interactions. *Sex Roles*, 50(7/8), 481-489.

ARE U CUMMING?

When a co-worker says to me, "Suck my big, fat cock," my response is thankful, as I sit there and ponder on the marketing approach I'm going to focus on that day. It doesn't offend me, since I work at a sexual "health and wellness" manufacturing company and discuss sex 8/5. It's a much different position than my former occupation as a high school teacher. If a kid said, "Suck it," I was required to send him down to the principal's office for his inappropriate behavior. That poor kid wouldn't stand a week of employment where I work now. In the adult industry people get fired for censoring themselves. Appropriate behavior **is** inappropriate behavior!

That last part isn't exactly the truth. But the reality is that the range of acceptable behavior at my current workplace is much broader than the public school system. And that's because of two reasons: 1) We are in the adult business, and 2) the personalities in this field of work are very permissive. It doesn't mean that the company I work for doesn't have professional conduct standards, or that my co-workers and I don't have professional working relationships. It simply means that we are accustomed to working in an uncensored atmosphere, are extremely nonjudgmental, and aren't offended by the majority of sexual terms or behaviors. Does that mean sexual harassment cannot happen at a place like this? FUCK NO! Just the other day, I was reading about a cocktail server who was suing the strip club that she worked for! Sexual harassment lawsuits can happen at anytime, anywhere! So beware! *Beware!!!*

What is sexual harassment? Sexual harassment qualifies as unwanted advances, suggested sexual favor, physical or verbal harassment. It is basically any "unwanted" sexual behavior. *Well, what the hell does that mean?!?!?* Exactly...

Like porn, there is no exact definition when it comes to sexual harassment. It is in the eye of the beholder. Technically, if you're flirting with someone for whatever motivation, i.e., exploration, instrumental, etc., you're taking a risk on possibly sexually harassing that person. What happens if a) Your flirtee is not only uninterested in you, but b) they're also offended by the way you flirted!?! You'd better hope they don't have the time and the money to buy a lawyer. Cause sometimes it's as simple as that!

Luckily, when you get involved in a sexual harassment claim, it doesn't go straight to a lawsuit. The unwanted affair is usually brought to a higher power's attention, i.e., a principal or supervisor. Then, it is their job to make the appropriate measurements to ensure that the uncomfortable advances don't happen again. Either way, if you're the one who caused the problem, you're fucked.

Sexual harassment in the workplace is the most emphasized. It's because businesses play their part as educators, so if an incident occurs, they can't be legally blamed. If you are harassed at work, you have a higher chance of being harassed by a co-worker than a superior. (This is good in case they're *really* an asshole. Cause it's easier to get them fired if they're not your boss.) The industries with the highest amount of sexual harassment are as follows: Finance, sales, marketing, hospitality, civil service, and education. You'd think they'd have food and beverage listed listed too, considering that every person on the staff has slept with your server.

Sexual harassment doesn't have to take place specifically

at work. It can also happen at school, Boy Scouts, the ice-skating rink, or even at home! If anyone makes sexual advances at you and it makes you feel uncomfortable-sexual harassment it is! The difficulty lies within deciphering where the line is crossed. If you're five and your six-year-old neighbor is asking you to drop your pants for a check-up, you can best guess that they haven't completed their MCAT yet, but is this an example where the parents should get involved and file suit? If a male leans towards his female co-worker every morning, sniffs, and tells her that her hair smells great, is that sexual harassment? Well, perhaps if he's a midget! Or excuse me… A little person.

Let's face it: Sexual harassment happens every day! When you were younger, you were "bullied". But guess what, Kids? It doesn't go away! When you're older you're bullied too! But the majority of the bullying for adults consists of R-rated verbiage, classifying it as sexual harassment. Either way, it happens. But always know that if you're the victim of sexual harassment, it's NOT your fault. (Unless you're sexting someone and one of your phones get into the wrong hands. Then, it's partially your fault. Don't want your dick being published all over the internet? Stop leaving proof of your undersized yogurt shooter.) Sure, a fish is going to feel more harassed than a dolphin on a regular basis; but, it really doesn't matter how thick your skin is. If you feel harassed, you're feeling hurt, offended, or intimidated. Does the offender *mean* to make you feel that way? It really doesn't matter! The point is that you DO feel that way, and no one deserves to feel harassed. So, if you ever encounter sexual bullying, do your first job: Communicate your negative feelings to the perpetrator. And if they don't stop? Do your second: Go get help!

Going back to the fish and the dolphin statement, different things are going to offend different people. If someone spreads a rumor around school that Haley is a slut for getting caught giving Justin a blowjob in the bathroom at a party Saturday night, she's probably going to feel embarrassed by all of the stares she receives in the hallways. But you never know! There's a slight chance that Haley feeds off that attention and doesn't mind the fact that everyone knows of her sexual exploitation! Perhaps, she's an underdeveloped exhibitionist! On the other hand, if Jared is referred to as a "three through seven" by one of his teammates, and he's actually gay, it may spark anger and hurt; which in turn, might end in a fist fight... Which may ALSO turn into a lawsuit...

Yes, one of the morals of this chapter is 'Not to piss off the wrong person'. But you'll have a much less chance of getting into trouble if you keep your eyes and mind open, and pay attention to how others react to your words and actions. Not everyone sees things the way you intend them. Let's talk sexting, shall we?

Sexting occurs when you send sexually explicit material (words or visuals) via cell phone or other electronic devices. This is all fun and games until you take a cleavage photo of the girl sitting next to you in History class and send it to your teammates. Because when that one kid gets caught texting in class and gets his phone confiscated, guess who's going to get arrested? You! Oh! Did I mention that you'll also be branded as a sex offender for life? Take a good, long hard look at that cleavage shot; cause it's going to be the last time you see any titties any time soon...

It doesn't even matter if the girl is your consenting girlfriend. If she's underage, you're fucked. That principal's going to get that photo and make a decision on how blown out of proportion this whole scenario is going to get. That's why you always need to be careful when texting someone else. The original intent of a text message or email is very difficult interpret. You may be thinking right now, *That's ridiculous! I always understand the intent and voice behind the text messages sent to my phone!* But what if you were reading someone else's messages and trying to decipher if something inappropriate was being said or done?

You get a text: "What time r u cumming home?"
You answer: "Right now."
Your response: "I'm so tired..."
You answer back: "I'll wake you up when I get home."
You get a smiley face...
Five minutes later: "Are you cumming yet?"
Then, a wink...

Does your girlfriend want to fuck you before she falls asleep? Perhaps. Or maybe your mom is waiting for her New Year's Eve date (her son) for the evening and doesn't know what the incorrect spelling of "coming" really means! What if you're receiving these messages from your baby-sitter waiting for you to get home? Textual harassment? Maybe! It depends if they're hot or not!

According to Saturday Night Live, the three simple rules to avoiding a sexual harassment lawsuit are: 1) Be handsome, 2) be attractive, and 3) don't be unattractive. Let's face it; if you're good-looking, you may make certain lawsuits look hot! (It's not mean if it's true... Well, on second thought; I guess it could be both...) Just remember, people don't always take things the way you intended them to be. Our primary goal is to have happy pandas! Not sad...

References:

AdamSlowHandSmith. "Tom Brady on SNL Skit (Smigel): 'Sexual Harassment and You'. Online video clip. *Youtube*. YouTube, 14, Nov. 2009. Web. July 10, 2013.

Association of Women for Action and Research. (2013). Statistics. *Workplace Sexual Harassment*. Retrieved from http://www.aware.org.sg/ati/wsh-site/14-statistics/

Burnside, J. (2011, Oct 2). New Teen Sexting Law Now in Effect. *NBC News*. Retrieved from http://www.nbcmiami.com/news/Teen-Sexting-Law-130902588.html

Nemours. (2013). Sexual harassment and sexual bullying. Retrieved from http://kidshealth.org/teen/school_jobs/bullying/harassment.html

Schram, J. (2013, June 14). Nix to sex got me fired: $5M Scores suit. *New York Post*. Retrieved from http://www.nypost.com/p/news/local/manhattan/nix_to_sex_got_me_fired_scores_suit_1q5lUFlSx0pKMwdOcDh8GK

"Sexual Harassment Panda". *South Park*. Comedy Central. CTV, New York City. 17 July,1999. Television.

U.S. Equal Employment Opportunity Commission. (n.d.). Sexual harassment. Retrieved from http://www.eeoc.gov/laws/types/sexual_harassment.cfm

University of Oregon. (2010). Sexual harassment: Myths and realities. Retrieved from http://counseling.uoregon.edu/dnn/SelfhelpResources/SexualAssaultSexualAbuse/SexualHarassmentMythsandRealities/tabid/390/Default.aspx

MÉNAGE À PAW

While sitting around a bonfire with my friends discussing our versions of hell, I simply declared, "Mine would be watching puppies being endlessly tortured." The only other version of hell that made me contemplate changing my answer was my friends: "My version of hell would consist of me rowing down a river of beer... Of which... I cannot drink.... With penises of all shapes and sizes, floating around me... Of which... I cannot fuck.... And the aroma of pot... Of which I cannot smoke." I'll admit, I did rethink my answer, but stuck with the tortured puppies. Perhaps, living on the edge of the cove in Taiji, Japan would be equally as horrifying; either way, for those of you who want to show your support, text "dolphin" to 44144.

I once heard that twenty-seven percent of people who grow up on a farm have their first sexual experience with a farm animal. (Please read the following question REALLY SLOWLY:) What the fuck? (I'm just sayin...) When I first heard this, I realized why I don't really get along with people who like country music. *Well, obviously, it's because they're all animal rapists!* But in all seriousness, if you *did* grow up on a farm, and you mouth the phrase, "I love animals," be sure to top it off with, "they taste delicious!" Otherwise, you may be confused as a chicken fucker, instead of a chicken lover.

It is assumed that people who have sex with animals have

below average intelligence and are from rural areas. Even though the frequency of contact is higher amongst people with lower educational achievement, research reveals this is not always the case. There are plenty of people that have sexual experiences with animals who have valid IQ levels and who outwardly appear moralistic.

A large-scale, general population study implemented by Alfred Kinsey found that 8% of men admitted having a sexual experience with an animal. Most of these experiences occurred at pre-pubescent ages with peaks around the ages of 10-12. The research showed a drastic drop in adult bestiality episodes, but get this: 26% of college rural males reached point of orgasm during their bestiality experiences. I know what you're thinking, *There are country folk that have been accepted into college?!?!?*

I recently saw a child get licked in the face by a dog and yell, "Ew! Its tongue went in my mouth!" I laughed and thought, *Ha! Your first French kiss was with a dog.* And I was right! This child had a sexual experience with a dog! This thought was followed by a look of disgust, as I realized that I have too... Why? Because dogs' tongues are slippery little suckers, and they're QUICK! And for those of us who actually believe the crock of shit statement that a dog's mouth is cleaner than a human's, and allow dogs to give us kisses on the mouth; well, we deserve an anal smelling tongue to make its way past our teeth. That right there, my Friends, is a sexual experience with an animal. So, next time you're playing *Never Have I Ever* and someone says, "Had a sexual experience with an animal." You'd better drink, mother fucker-DRINK!

As natural as the slip of a dog's tongue may be; to many people, bestiality is a disgusting, unbearable act. Interspecies sexual interactions are comparable to acts like abusing women and pedophilia. This is because having sex with an animal can hurt or kill it. They're a different species than we are, so that's just weird! And an important thing to remember is that animals don't speak. (Well, they don't speak our language; other than Mishka, that talking Husky on *Youtube*.) So, having sex with them is a non-consensual act. Or is it?

A guy is railing a woman from behind and feels something strange on his ball sack. He glances back to find her eight-week kitten pawing at his wiggling pouch. He has a choice to make: Does he pull out, grab the kitten, and remove it from the scene? Or does he laugh it off, and continuing pounding his woman?

A man and two women are going at it. He decides it would be extra entertaining if he were to place some whip cream on Girl A's poonanny and watch Girl B lick it off. After Girl B licks the majority of it off, she starts giving the guy a blow job while the cream is in her mouth. As she's going at it, his greyhound walks over to Girl A's crotch to lick up some of the sweet remnants. Girl A shockily enjoys the cunnalingus and is surprised to realize that the dog is better at giving head than Girl B.

A woman lives in Hawaii. She is in the midst of her daily swim in a nearby cove with a familiar pod of dolphins. She notices a male calf with an erection is swimming fairly close to her. She continues to smoothly swim side by side in hopes that he comes closer. The beauty of the animal is so overwhelming, that when he comes inches from her body and she feels its S-shaped penis touch her genital area, she is overcome with ecstasy.

Whether you feel as though these illustrations are examples of sexual perversions or sexual deviations, it doesn't change the fact these things happen. And the disclaimer is that no animals were harmed in the above examples. Unfortunately, the reality is that there are plenty of dog corpses that the ASPCA comes across due to cruel bestiality acts; but, if the animal chooses to participate in the sexual act should the human participant be arrested for partaking in the interspecies sexual activity?

Most of you are probably angrily screaming in your heads right now, "YES!" But you'd be shocked to know how many people actually have experienced pretty raunchy sex shit with animals. It is rare for a person to have a sexual *preference* for animals over humans, but sometimes people are so enthralled in the sexcapade that when the animal jumps on in, they think, "Eh…what the hell?!" This zoophilic act is usually followed with insane amounts of guilt, as these instances are not socially acceptable in our culture. Therefore, if your best friend used to use the slime off her frog's back for masturbation lubrication when she was younger, she probably won't be the first to let the cat out of the bag and share her animalistic sexual experience.

Please read the following excerpt from a 14-year-old girl's diary about the new man in her life:

> Today was the most amazing day ever! I've been waiting for it my entire life! When I saw him, I knew I had to have him. He was beautiful. Dark, tall and handsome, with luscious, layered black hair and eyes as dark and magical as an abyss. When I introduced myself and he made no sound. He just looked deep into my soul. It gave me goosebumps and I felt a rise of energy build up inside of me that made me want to burst. As he continued to stare, I became extremely shy and realized that as docile as he was acting, he was claiming dominance at that very moment. After standing silently for minutes on end, I reached my hand out and ran my fingers through his hair. He nuzzled his face up against mine and I knew it was time. I mounted him and felt his strength between my legs. I felt as though we were one. That first ride will forever be etched into my brain. I am so in love.

Prime example of anthromorphism or personification? Perhaps. But you can't deny the fact that it's not that abnormal for a human to feel an emotional and physical attraction to an animal. How one chooses to act upon it is a different matter. For some, they illegally participate in sexual activities with animals. Others fear that they'll end up like Mr. Hands, so they downplay and dress up as furries or partake in pony play! Who knows!?!? Perhaps the list of sexual minorities will soon add on another letter for zoosexual orientation: LGBTQZ! At this rate, if we keep adding categories, sexual minorities-they will be no more!

References:

Beetz, A. M. (2004). Bestiality/Zoophilia: A scarcely investigated phenomenon between crime, paraphilia and love. *Journal of Forensic Psychology Practice*, 4(2), 1-36.

Beirne, P. (2000). Rethinking bestiality: Towards a concept of interspecies sexual assault. In A. Podberscek,E. Paul, J. Serpell (Eds.), *Companion animals and us: Exploring the relationships between people and pets*. New York, NY: Cambridge University Press.

Duffield, G., Hassiotis, A. & Vizard, Eillen. (1998). Zoophilia in young sexual abusers. *Journal of Forensic Psychiatry*, 9(2), 294-304.

Earls, C. M. & Lalumiere, M.L. (2009). A case study of preferential bestiality. *Archives of Sexual Behavior*, 38(4), 605-609.

Gardea23. (2008, February 7). *Husky Dog Talking-"I love you"*. Retrieved December 22, 2012, from http://lynn.libguides.com/content. php?pid=47000&sid=349970

London, L. S. & Caprio, F. S. (1960). *Sexual deviations*. Washington, DC: The Linacre Press.

WHO'S YOUR DADDY?!?!

John is a twenty-four year old man who is a pre-school teacher, in the midst of getting his master's degree in Elementary Education. On a Tuesday afternoon, he finds himself at the front office with one of his students who is searching through the crowd of parents looking for his father. The child points and mumbles something that John can't quite hear. "Who's your Daddy?" John asks. The boy points to a man, and seconds later John is relieved to safely unite the father and son. Later that evening, John's railing his girlfriend in a hot and heated session. "Who's your Daddy?!?!" John yells. For a split second, John gets a disturbing shock in his head, as he recalls saying the same words to a four year old boy earlier in the day. *Fuck it.* He thinks… And continues to bang the shit out of her.

The term, "Who's your Daddy?!?!" dates back to 1909 when the term "daddy" was used in a blues song to indicate a pimp. Since then, "daddy" has become established in African American speech to describe a male lover. Now, we hear the terms "Sugar Daddy", referring to someone who has money; "Jailhouse Daddy", referring to the dominant person in a homosexual relationship; and even "Smack Daddy" referring to Obama. It is evident that "daddy" refers to a variety of personas, other than the male parental figure in your life. But here's my question: If you're one of the many who like yelling the term, "Who's your Daddy?!?!" in the bedroom, are you ever concerned that your partner may NOT be turned on by that phrase? Because personally, if someone brings up one of my family members in the sack, I'm going to dry up like unmilked cereal.

Incest. It happens! Usually when the topic comes up, the first thing that crosses someone's mind is West Virginia. Personally, I'm surprised the punch line of every incest joke isn't New Jersey; considering the fact that everyone is born and raised. The other example that comes to mind is rape. This stems from the fact that 43% of child sexual abuse is done by a family member. And since the media revolves child rape around pedophilia, people usually associate incestuous behavior with dirty, mustached uncles, or crippled stepfathers. Surprisingly enough, the most common type incest, yet the least reported, occurs when siblings are playing "pretend". Sure, there's always the accidental case where you go to a costume party, and end up playing *7 Minutes in Heaven* with your brother in a dark closet; but in reality, it is far more prevalent for incest to occur between siblings than adult-to-child incest. In fact, a comparison study revealed that 70.8% of sibling incest goes as far as penetration; whereas, only 27% of stepfather incest and 35% of father incest reached the penetration stage. This may have something to do with size… I'm just sayin'.

Incest doesn't just happen with children. Even mature adults allow themselves to fall in love and fuck someone who is genetically similar. This isn't so farfetched considering that people are more attracted to faces that resemble their own. Well, usually the person who looks most like you is your sibling. I bet all of you, "only-child"s, are sighing in relief. But no worries! You're still in luck, and can have some incestuous fun if you have a cousin! In fact, not only can you have sex with your cousin, but you can marry them too! There are plenty of states that allow first cousin marriages; New Jersey, being one of them. And get this: West Virginia IS NOT! Why the hell does West Virginia have such an incestuous reputation? It turns out that its breeding stereotype is linked back to the state's poverty history. Lame, I know. Sorry

I couldn't provide more entertaining gossip on the Mountain State... But, let's go back to cousin fucking, shall we?!?!?

The reason why our country is lax on laws regarding cousin marriages, but not sibling marriages is because of the danger of reproduction between siblings. When a child is made, half its chromosomes come from its father; the other half comes from its mother. If a defective gene is located on the mother's side, usually the father's set of genes will take over and the defective gene will not be passed on to the child. If siblings are procreating and a defective, or deleterious, gene appears, the chances that it's on both copies of the chromosomes are extremely high. This will result in the child getting the defective gene. And if that's the case, many shitty phenotypes could occur; but, then again, two siblings can also produce a perfectly healthy offspring!

Let's look at the animal kingdom, shall we? Animals have incest all of the time! It's called inbreeding. Is your dog pure-bred? If not, its parents very well may have been related. Limited evidence does support the fact that animals prefer not to mate within the family; so, if they have a preference, they'll usually choose to mate with another set of genes. But they still do sex shit to each other all of the time! I have two dogs who are sisters. They're constantly licking each other's genitals. I know they're not performing oral because they're horny-but come on! It's not like they're NOT getting pleasure from getting their pussies licked! Why do they do it? Because they don't give a shit! Animals don't have guilt after having a sexual encounter with a family member because they don't see incest as immoral. Well, humans are animals too! Aside from the fact that reproducing with a family member will dramatically increase the chances of birth defects, why is society so against it? Aren't we all a result from our inbred ancestors?

We could blame it on our cultures and the fact that we grow up with the idea that giving your father a blow job is frowned upon. But according to the Westermarck Hypothesis, created by

Edward Westermarck, humans who grow up in close quarters develop an aversion to sexual activities with each other. He suggests that the repugnance that we develop during childbirth is what makes us develop the mentality that incest is taboo; therefore, our disgust in incest can be blamed on our innate mindset, not society's moral outrage.

Whatever your position is, I'm going to end this chapter with a little, "WHAT IF" scenario: You meet the person of your dreams at the age of twenty-five. You move in two years later, and are engaged by the age of twenty-nine. You can't imagine your life without this person; they are your second half... Literally. You find out during your blood test two weeks before the wedding that you're siblings.

Do you stay together? Why don't you marinate on that for a little while?

References:

Carlson, B.E., Maciol, K., & Schneider, J. (2006). Sibling incest: Reports from forty-one survivors. *Journal of Child Sexual Abuse*, 15(4), 19-34. doi: 10.1300/J070v15n04_02

Cyr, M., Wright, J., McDuff, P., & Perron, A. (2002). Intrafamilial sexual abuse: Brother-sister incest does not differ from father-daughter and stepfather-stepdaughter incest. *Child Abuse & Neglect*, 26(9), 957-974.

Farhi, P. (2005, January 4). Conception of a question: Who's your daddy? *Washington Post*. Retrieved from http://www.washingtonpost.com/wp-dyn/articles/A46032-2005Jan3.html

Harvey, P.H. & Ralls, K. (1986). Do animals avoid incest? *Nature*, 320(6063), 575-576. doi: 10.1038/320575b0

Lapidos, J. (2008, June 3). West Virginia, incest Virginia? How the Mountain State got a reputation for inbreeding. Retrieved from http://www.slate.com/articles/news_and_politics/explainer/2008/06/west_virginia_incest_virginia.html

Minkel, J. (2010, September 17). Freud was (half) right about incest. Retrieved from http://www.livescience.com/10107-freud-incest.html

National Conference of State Legislatures. (2012). *State Laws Regarding Marriages Between First Cousins*. Retrieved from http://www.ncsl.org/issues-research/human-services/state-laws-regarding-marriages-between-first-cousi.aspx

Shor, E. & Simchai, D. (2009). Incest avoidance, the incest taboo, and social cohesion: revisiting Westermarck and the case of Israeli kibbutzim. *AJS*, 114(6), 1803-1842.

DOES 'NO' REALLY MEAN 'NO'?

Last night my boyfriend picked me up from my house. He went to open the car door for me, and sitting on my passenger seat was a beautiful, red rose. We went out to dinner, and laughed the entire time. The wine was flowing and I felt like I was falling in love all over again. Afterwards, we took a romantic walk on the beach. As the clouds covered the moon, he grabbed me close, looked me deep in the eyes, and with his hand upon my cheek said, "I'm so in love with you, Babe." We began to kiss and when the rain droplets started hitting our skin, we didn't budge. Nothing was going to interrupt what we had going.

As our bodies became engrossed in the moment, neither of us instigated dropping down to the sand, as we both knew would have been a hot mess. We started running back to the car, laughing; and when we arrived, he grabbed my body and he kissed me. I wrapped my legs around him as he sat me down on the hood of the car. He started kissing down my body, and then started going down on me. At the second, when I arched my back and screamed, I thought I couldn't have a more exhilarating experience. I was wrong…. He entered me. I grabbed his neck and we stared endlessly into each other's eyes. I felt as though we were one, and nothing else in the world mattered. I can't even begin to tell you how intense my orgasm was; and what made it even better was simultaneously seeing him cum at the same time. Exhausted and deliriously satisfied, we held each other in the pouring rain. He got up on the hood with me, and I snuggled my head in his arm, thanking God for such a perfect match.

So, I was at the club with my girls, scanning the crowd for the pick of the evening, and I saw the hottest piece of ass ever! I made my way over to him and we chatted it up for two hours. I was in love! Not only did I know I was going to screw his brains out, I thought to myself, "This guy *could actually be* boyfriend material!" As a respectable decision, I decided NOT to sleep with him that night. Instead, I coaxed him into asking me out for Friday night. When Friday night came, he took me out to a restaurant for dinner and we had the most sexually stimulating conversation. I don't remember the last time I was so turned on; I would have taken him on the dinner table right there if my mom wasn't friends with the owner of the place. When the sex conversation came up, he responded with, "I've done it all." I doubted him for a moment, but then he continued, "—from threesomes to golden showers…"

"Damn!" I though. "I've got to step up my game!" Excited, I invited him back to my place for dinner the following evening. When he kissed me goodnight, I felt so proud that I was holding out until the third date. The following morning, I went to the store, and bought expensive ingredients to make a schmancy dinner. I set the table, worked out and started getting ready. When he showed up at my house, I sat him down and poured the wine. We had great conversation; it was so obvious we were skipping out on desert. He went to pick up our dishes to put them in the sink, and as he came back, he leaned over and kissed me; although, our kissing did not stop there. Through the kitchen, up the stairs, and to my room we went. I shoved him on the bed and told him to close his eyes.

"I have a surprise for you," I said. He eagerly did as I asked. I blindfolded him, took the remainder of his clothes off, and handcuffed him to the bed. He was definitely liking the way things were going. I stripped down to nothing and got on top of him. Kissing him up and down, I finally stood up over him, and waited. Scared, but kind of excited, I started to pee. I only planned on giving him a trickle; but, it just so turns out, when you start to pee; it's really hard to stop!

"What the hell are you doing?" he screamed.

"Sorry!" I yelled, but there was no use. My pee was running down his torso, onto my mattress. I finally jumped off the bed, and let him lose as he was violently thrashing around.

"What the hell?" he yelled angrily at me.

"I thought you liked this kind of stuff… Last night at dinner-"

"I was joking! Seriously?!?! You seriously thought—" he gave me one last look of disbelief, grabbed his clothes, and walked out. Needless to say, I never saw him again.

Oh well… There's a first for everything!

It's been four months. I still hate myself every day. It was October 14th, and I went with my best friend to a fraternity party. We were supposed to meet up with seven other people, but they never showed. I suppose they got caught up at a different party. Well, my friend and I were enjoying ourselves, and when the keg stands started happening… I remember feeling like I was slipping. Slipping into darkness, I guess because after a few of them, I blacked out.

The next morning, I woke up in some guy's bed. There were clothes thrown all around the room. I quickly started scouring the room for clues. Did I even know this guy? As I grabbed my bra, I found a condom… The first one. It was thrown on the floor, obviously used, but there was no cum inside. I felt a strange feeling of relief. *Well, I guess we used protection, and he didn't finish. I'm sure I'm fine.* Turning my head towards the bed, I noticed another condom near the pillow. Empty again. I turned on the light switches to get help finding the rest of my stuff, but yelped when a third condom dropped from the ceiling fan right in front of my face. This one was not empty. Disgusted and ready to puke, I grabbed my shoes and ran out the room, passing another used condom on the dresser. This one too, was not empty. I hurried into the kitchen, where three guys were making eggs and bacon. "Hey!" One of them said with a smile. "Want some breakfast?"

"No," I abruptly answered. The other one looked up at me with a bewildered look on his face, "Last night was crazy, huh?"

I stared at him, trying NOT to puke all over their kitchen floor. "Uh, I have to go…"

As I turned towards the door to walk out, one of them yelled behind me, "Hey! Do you need any money for a taxi?"

"No!" I yelled as I ran out the door.

I have no clue what happened that night. I have no clue if I had sex; and if so, who I slept with, and how many people I slept with. Humiliated and ashamed, to this day, I have never told a single soul what may have happened that night. I want to get tested, but I'm afraid.

People share their sex stories. Usually the ones that are told around the bonfire over a couple of beers are the funny ones. And your best bud might share the amazing experience that he and his girl had on their weekend getaway. But it's rare for someone to honestly open up and share a sex horror story. Whether it's because they are ashamed, in denial, or just plain scared; the reality that most of us seem to forget is that everyone has had a best sexual experience, everyone has had a funniest sexual experience, and everyone has had a worst sexual experience.

A girl goes to a party and has *no* intentions of having sex. She gets wasted and starts making out with some guy. He pulls his cock out and tries to slip it up her skirt. She declines playfully by pushing it away, but proceeds to sloppily make out with him. He tries again. She says, "No," and the making out continues.

"Come on…" he tries to coax her. A few minutes later, his dick is pressing up her pussy.

"No," she says again. "We really shouldn't!" She feels the tip enter her body. "No—" she whispers, as he kisses her and shushes her. She reluctantly kisses him back and continues to do so more heavily, as he thrusts himself inside of her.

The next morning she wakes up naked next to him on the couch. Recalling the night before, she becomes overwhelmed with guilt and regret. She states the solemn vow: *I will never drink again...*

Who's at fault here?

Well, let's look at the facts. She *said*, "No!" But the guy didn't take her seriously. Did she really mean 'no'? Or was she just playing the innocent role? Perhaps, the meaning behind her "no" was to suggest, "No. You're going to have to do some more convincing than that." Whatever the reason, she verbally declined. She also declined by physically pushing his dick aside; but her effort wasn't assertive enough for him to get the picture. Or did he get the picture and just didn't give two shits about what she wanted? Or did he not; because, he too, was wasted? Oh yeah! And then there's the alcohol factor, which really doesn't help the situation. And you wonder why your parents get nervous when you tell them you're going to an unsupervised party on Friday night.

Best case scenario: He asks her out the following day, and they eventually become a couple. They continue to go to parties together and have passionate, protected sex, until the day comes when they get happily married, buy a dog, a house, and have three kids.

Worst case scenario: She gets knocked up, and drops out of school. For months, her parents threaten to press charges against the boy, but decide against it for the baby's sake. He loses his scholarship and never attends college. The parents of the kid who threw the party get sued, resulting in the kid putting a bullet in his head because of the guilt he has from dragging his parents through the legal drama. Twenty years later, the two of them are grandparents because their sixteen year old daughter got banged up and is pregnant with her second child. They're still born and raised in the same town, with no college education, making little-to-no money, and miserable. They claim the best time in their lives was their high school years, *before* the night of the party.

Probable case scenario: She sneaks out of the house, anxiously awaits her next period, and the two of them awkwardly exchange looks in the hallways of school. The two of them pretend like the night never happened until they meet up at another party during Spring Break, five years later, where they drunkingly decide to have another fuck; for old time's sake.

No matter which alternate ending you choose, we still haven't discussed who's *fault* the unwanted sexual encounter was. His', hers', or both of theirs'? Or we can take the easy way out by choosing the notorious scapegoat and blame it on the al-al-al-al-al-al-cohol.

Alcohol is bad Kids, m'kay? Sixty percent of women who have contracted a sexually transmitted infection were drunk at the time of infection. Wow. Just think. If none of those women allowed themselves to "over-indulge", they would have possibly used a condom at the time, and would be STI-free!

I know what you're thinking! "Wait a second, TayloR! That statistic said nothing about those women being condomless. How do you know they didn't use a condom?" Well, you're right! I'm completely speculating. But get this: Not only does alcohol cloud your judgment, but it increases vulnerability, sexual aggression and risky behavior; hence why, while under the influence of alcohol, people are **three times** as likely to *not* use protection! Although, people have more fear of "date drugs" being slipped into their drink, what they need to pay more attention to is what's actually IN their drink already! Alcohol is the most prevalent date drug. If someone plans on asserting themselves sexually on their date at the end of the evening, they're much more likely to keep feeding them drinks and buying more rounds than slipping a Mexican Valium (Rohypnol), Liquid Ecstasy (GHB), or a Kit Kat (Ketamine) in their beverage! But, if you're more than welcome to have your significant other get you wasted before they take you home and have their way with you, than you're not a rape victim… Just a drunk.

Aside from gang rape, spousal rape, or prison rape, the rape teens are most used to hearing about is date rape because 57% of rapes occur on a date! Let's take a moment and think about this. When you go out on a date, are you on guard? Do you pack your pepper spray? Now compare how you react on a date to when you're walking home alone at nighttime. You're probably more alert and concerned during your walk home, as opposed to your date. This is because the thought of a strange man jumping out of the bushes and attacking you when no one else is around is more frightening than your date trying to push themselves on you. That, and movies, television and news have highlighted "stranger danger" throughout the years. Funny though… You never see a kid yelling "*acquaintance* danger".

*Just a side note if any of you ever find yourself in the position where someone is attacking you or attempting to rape you, FIGHT BACK! For all of you Ladies that have it in your heads that you're just going to act all into it, chances are the raper will not stop. If they've gone that far, they're not just going to stop, get up and walk away; they're going to finish what they've started. Yes, if you fight back, the chances that you are injured are increased by ten percent; but, if you fight back, the odds of you being raped are cut in half. (Fingernails are a great weapon. Aim for the eyes.)

Moving along, another commonly used term that teens are warned about is statutory rape. This term is used to describe sexual activities that take place between one person and another person who is below the age of legal consent. The age of legal consent ranges from 16-18 years old, depending on what state you live in. And the laws in each state can be extremely intricate; check out Washington State, for example: The age of consent in

Washington is 16 years old; but that doesn't mean that if you're under the age of 16 you can't have sex. In fact, you're more than welcome to have sex, but it has to be with someone of the right age. In Washington State, sex with an underage person is **not** considered rape if the age differences between the two willing participants are the follows: 2 (if the younger participant is < 12), 3 (if the younger participant is < 14), 4 (if the younger participant is < 16). What this means is that a twelve year old and a fourteen year old can have sex. Even a nine year old and eleven year old! But, if a nine year old and a thirteen year old were to get frisky, it would be considered statutory rape. As for the sixteen year olds, they can fuck whoever they'd like, **EXCEPT** for a K-12 teacher, a police officer, or someone who has custodial care over them, i.e., a registered nurse or pyschiatrist. HOWEVER! It is completely acceptable for a sixteen year old to fuck their local firemen! *Sweet.*

If you're questioning yourself in jest, wondering if you're are a rape victim, because your significant other is three years older than you, or wondering how ironic it would be to be raped while *Nirvana* is being played in the background; step away from the light for a moment and take a look down the dark alleyway. Going back to the fact that everyone has a "worst sexual experience", count your blessings if your worst involved a consensual act. If *your* worst was when your parents walked in on you and you were right about to impregnate your girlfriend's mouth; be thankful; because, whether or not people who have had a non-consensual sexual experience call it "rape"; it happens. Every two minutes someone is sexually assaulted in the United States. Whether that assault consists of full-on rape or not, we can at least determine that every two minutes, a "worst sexual experience" is being created; and that, my Friends, is something that no one deserves.

The majority of the time rape is discussed, the example being used involves a woman being raped by a man. This is because it is a more common scenario. Plain and simple: 99% of rapists are men. But men get raped too! Not only is it possible for a man to get raped by a woman, what happens even more is a man getting raped by another man. The U.S. Centers for Disease Control report that 4% of men have experienced a sexual act against their will. So whether this act occurred when they were a child, from someone who accompanied them on a romantic evening, or at a gay club; men should not be stereotyped as rapists. They too, are victims.

John is putzin' down a hallway of his high school. In one of the rooms, there is a Women's Studies class in session. All participants in the room are freshmen and female. The professor has just completed an intense lesson on date rape; without indicating the sex of either the rapist or the victim. No gender specific pronouns for either role were used; instead, the labels "the rapist" and "the victim" were constantly referred to. The lesson ended while the boy was walking past the classroom. As the teacher saw his face walk past the window, she ran out of the classroom and asked a favor of him. The boy followed the teacher back into the room. He stopped and stood in the center of the class. "Now Ladies?" the professor asks for the girls' attention. "This is John. He is a white seventeen year-old male, and a fellow peer that attends this school. He is an honor roll student and the catcher for your Varsity baseball team. This Friday evening he is going out on a date. Describe his intentions." The class stares at John. "Go ahead," the teacher encourages the girls. "Just yell your thoughts out."

The girls continue to stare defiantly; as John realizes he's being glared at by a large group of angry females. The silence begins to make him sweat, until one of them breaks it by crossly muttering the word, "Asshole".

The girls begin to yell out angry comments and questions, "How far do you think you'll get with her?"

"I'm sure he'll be aiming for a homerun—"

"What are you going to do if she says, 'No'?"

"Do you EVEN KNOW WHAT 'NO' MEANS!?"

"Well, he's a *baseball* player—no one's going to say 'no' to him!" Someone yelled out sarcastically.

"Are you going to call her the next day?"

John stood like a deer in headlights and took the angry sarcastic remarks as if he was getting pelted with frozen paintballs. He caught the eye of one girl who stood out from the rest. She was sitting in the far back corner and looked at him with sad eyes, as if to apologize for putting him through the feminist attack.

The teacher noted the women getting louder and more riled up. "Ok," she yelled. "Thank you, Ladies!" The girls quieted down. The teacher turned to John. "Thank you, John. Would you please share with us how you feel after being accused of all of those things?"

John stood and looked at the girls. He shrugged. "Um…" he stuttered. "Hurt? Hated? Upset? I don't think it's right that none of you even know me-" he again caught the eye of the girl in the back. "Well, *most* of you don't know me." John turned and looked at the teacher. "I was in a really good mood before you pulled me in here…." He paused. "Can I go now?"

The teacher nodded and turned to her desk to write a pass. She handed it to John and thanked him again. After John exited the room, the girls broke into an uproar of chatter to discuss their reactions to the powerful past five minutes of class. They shut up quickly when they were abruptly interrupted by Jenna, the girl in far back corner, who had stood up and was filled with rage. "You girls are a bunch of ignorant bitches!" she yelled. "John's gay! He's been dating my brother for two years! He's absolutely amazing! And you just made him feel like *shit*—for NO REASON!" Jenna walked out of the classroom, leaving a roomful of shocked expressions behind.

When it comes to sexuality, you can't assume anything about anyone. Yes, it's hard not to stereotype, but sexuality is power. And when someone endures a negative sexual experience, their sense of power can be drastically altered. Most of the time, they feel as though they lose power; or a piece of themselves has been taken. Even your best friend has probably not shared their deepest, darkest sexual secrets. 42% of people who are raped never tell anyone about it; so, whether it's your best friend, your significant other, or your mother, the chances that they come to you to share their story are slim to none. But do you blame them? Have *you* truly confided in someone with the deep details of your worst experience? Probably not.

The ball's in your court, my Friend. Instigate the dialogue. Because if you confide in someone and share your "worst sexual experience" ever, your loving effort could change their lives forever.

References:

Cooper, M.L. (2002). Alcohol use and risky behavior among college students and youth: Evaluating the evidence. *Journal of Studies on Alcohol* (Suppl. 14), 101-117.

Drinkaware.co.uk. (2012). Alcohol and one night stands. Retrieved from http://www.drinkaware.co.uk/alcohol-and-you/relationships/alcohol-and-one-night-stands

Ghiglieri, M. (n.d.). No Safe Place: Violence Against Women. PBS. Salt Lake City, Utah.

One in Four, Inc. (2012). How often does rape happen to women? Retrieved from http://www.oneinfourusa.org/statistics.php

Peterson, Z.D., Janssen, E., Heiman, J. R. (2010). The association between sexual aggression and HIV risk behavior in heterosexual men. *Journal of Interpersonal Violence*, 25(3), 538-556.

Sound Vision Foundation. (2012). Statistics on Teens. Retrieved from http://soundvision.com/Info/teens/stat.asp

U.S. Department of Health and Human Services. (2012) *Statutory Rape: A Guide to State Laws and Reporting Requirements.* Retrieved from http://aspe.hhs.gov/hsp/08/sr/statelaws/summary.shtml

U.S. Department of Health and Human Services Office on Women's Health. (2008). *Date rape drugs face sheet.* Retrieved from http://www.womenshealth.gov/publications/our-publications/fact-sheet/date-rape-drugs.cfm

Intimacy

This circle of sexuality revolves around
relationships. Its major components consist
of emotional and physical interactions
between people in different staged
relationships.

TUESDAY

For those of you who were born in a conventional family household, you're probably used to hearing your fortune being described as: You'll graduate from high school, go to college, where you'll meet the man/woman of your dreams, graduate with Honors, get a job, buy a house, get married, have three kids and a dog. Maybe some of you have an aunt or another adult in your family that strays a little on the love advice, "You have to kiss a lot of toads, until you find your frog." But adults usually don't tell you the truth about sexually explicit relationships. The reality of "love" for many people involves sleeping around for years, until they find someone that fits *the majority* of the boxes on their checklist. This so-called "catch" is usually chosen right around the time that the biological clock starts ticking. But this chapter is not about the winning catch; it's about the runner uppers. Yeah, I'm talking about your Mondays, Tuesdays, Wednesdays, etc.

What is a "hook-up"? Well, if you ask mature adults, more than half of them refer to the definition as an informal meeting. Younger people, on the other hand… Well, they don't disagree with them per se; they would just prefer to throw in the word, "sexual" at the beginning of that definition. This is because there has been a historical shift throughout our generations. Over the past century, social norms created by peers, psychological attachment, and psychological development, have molded a different perspective of intimacy.

Back to the question, "What is a 'hook-up'"—well, that depends on your social circle. Some will say this "no strings attached" relationship is any sexual activity without commitment or emotional attachment. Others will say it is anything from a kiss to oral. While many will distinguish whether intercourse falls into the category of "hooking-up" or not; others just don't give a fuck and refer to "hooking-up" as a drunken mistake. Whichever way you look at it, this ambiguous term happens. And it may happen to you!

I read this article recently by Rebecca Stinson. It went a little like this: Hooking-up has become the normative heterosexual act to do on college campuses. "Many citizens have become **alarmed** that this trend is indicative of moral decline in our culture..." Ha ha! This made me laugh my ass off. *Many citizens have become alarmed*?!?!? More like jealous! Do you know how *lucky* the Y Generation is to have "hooking-up" be socially acceptable? Let's dive into why one would aspire to have a hook-up, or in other terms, friend with benefits relationship (FWB/FWBR), fuck buddy (FB), cater-cousin, and so on...

Why would someone want a FWB? Well, people are horny! And if you've been hard up for long enough, you're going to pick from the low-hanging fruit on the tree. She may be a butterface, but that's ok, because the majority of hook-ups occur at nighttime.

He or she may be easy on the eyes and you enjoy spending time with them, but you would *never* marry them. If this is the case, you may want to maintain a "friendship" with this person even though you foresee no future. Many people will uphold a FWB relationship because they have fun with that person, like having sex with that person and truly cherish that person. And yet, the thought of a long-term relationship or potential thought of marriage with the FB is nonexistent.

There's also the classic case of the rebound. The good ol' saying, "You can't get over someone until you get under someone else" may work on the mind, but not the heart. So beware if someone's wiping the glass with you. These relationships are known to contain strong urges, but weak commitments.

Ah, the classic case of a drunken hook-up. There's at least one at every party. This is one of the reasons why you should always carry a condom. Because when drunkenness prevails, dicks will be whipped out and panties will drop. And the last thing alcohol is going to do is help you say, "Stop!"

One of the main reasons why a FWB relationship may develop is because it's just easy! If you have a friend who you are sexually attracted to, and the two of you are sexually competent, you may escalate your status of being a "friend" to being a "friend with benefits". And truth be told, if the two of you are ok without a more intimate label, or a monogamous commitment to each other, it can be a very liberating and happy experience. You don't have to worry about making them a priority, snuggling postsex-it's just strictly physical and fun... Until feelings begin to develop... Then, what seemed to be a drama-free relationship that you regularly turned to on rainy days warps into fucking hurricane!

According to Erik Erikson's psychosocial stages, when an adolescent is becoming an adult, they enter the Intimacy verses Isolation stage. It is during this stage that the person strives to form a loving, intimate relationship. They fear being alone; which is why many people settle for FWB relationships at this age. It camouflages the feeling of isolation, because someone is being physically intimate with them. And depending on how long the FWBR lasts, one or both of the participants may become dependent on the other. They forget that this what-seemed-to-be-a-committed-relationship was never an actual commitment at all! And when their fuck buddy attempts to simply say, "Ok, I'm done with you," it's a whole different story in the breaker-uppee's mind.

"What do you mean you're done with me?!?!? What did I do!?! I'm the perfect person for you! We laugh, we have fun, we go out to dinner, we confide in each other and WE HAVE GREAT SEX! Why don't you want me anymore!?!?!"

Truthfully, this person will probably never know why their fuck buddy doesn't want them anymore. And it's obvious that this person read WAY too much into this FWB relationship than they should have. Notice how this "hook-up" involved dinners. Just because they went out doesn't actually mean that they "went out". Here's a sign to know if you're a participant in a FWBR: If your FB only takes you out on Tuesdays, it's not because they have a crazy-busy schedule. It's because you've been assigned as his/her "Tuesday". You're simply a scheduled fuck.

Unlike FWBRs, if you're in a *serious* relationship with someone, it's much easier to be honest with them during your break-up. You gave them your all, and it didn't work out. In long, drawn-out committed relationships the root of the problems is usually obvious anyway. So, there's really no need to lie.

When you want to break-up with your fuck buddy... Well, that's a different story with a more abrupt ending. If you're not an asshole, you're probably not going to want to tell them why you're really terminating the relationship: "My ex broke up with her boyfriend; I met someone that I like better than you; You are starting to get annoying with all of your texts; You're starting to act like we're together or something, and that's *not* happening; You're crazy; I would never marry you in a million years; I'm bored with you; That sound you made last night when you orgasmed reminded me of my sister, and I never want to have sex with you again". And if that's the case, just do your best to douse the fire gently and move on. Fuck buddy break-ups usually end in lies, lies, and even more lies....

So next time you want to hook-up with someone and have a drama-free relationship, think again! **I'm not saying that hooking up is an unhealthy thing to do, but I *am* saying that a hook-up is an unhealthy relationship.** As long as you see it that way, you'll be just fine. Just be careful, because if you're in the Intimacy vs. Isolation phase, getting dumped as a girlfriend/boyfriend is hard; but, getting dumped as a fuck buddy can be even harder.

To finalize this topic, I would like to comment on one of the most common questions that is brought to my attention. "I'm hooking up with this person, and I have no clue where this is going! How do I find out if I'm just a fuck buddy or if they actually like me?"

Ah... Labeling. What a stupid social construct we, as Americans, must endure. If you are unsatisfied with the "unknown" status of your relationship, you must put your heart on the line in order to differentiate where you stand. My advice to you if the hooking-up is bringing you constant anxiety and more stress than pleasure, is to prepare yourself for rejection, and then simply ask! An effortless, "Where is this going?" will probably bring about a vague answer; but, if you let them know where you stand and honestly ask for reciprocation, you'll get an honest answer back. Here's a good one: "I really like you and I want to know if there's potential for this relationship getting more serious. If not; that's ok. I would just like to know, because I don't want to waste my time."

Don't try to justify why you're asking or reconfirm that you're "not talking about marriage or anything"... If that's the case, you'll just look like a pathetic dumbass. Simply and politely ask for clarification. You'll get it; and if not, well... They're just not that into you. In the meantime, while you're figuring it all out, just relax... And don't forget to use a condom! We don't want any bastard childs, now do we?!?

References:

Fortunato, L., Young, A.M., Boyd, C. J., & Fons, C. E. (2010). Hook-up sexual experiences and problem behaviors among adolescents. *Journal of Child & Adolescent Substance Abuse, 19*, 261-278.

Kooyman, L., Pierce, G., & Zavadil. (2011). Hooking up and identity development of female college students. *Adultspan Journal, 10*(1), 4-13.

Penhollow, T., Young, M., & Bailey, W. (2007). Relationship between religiosity and "hooking up" behavior. *American Journal of Health Education, 38*(6), 338-345.

Stinson, R. D. (2010). Hooking up in young adulthood: A review of factors influencing the sexual behavior of college students. *Journal of College Student Psychotherapy, 24*(2), 98-115.

'IN A RELATIONSHIP'

Dating… The process of courtship is extremely interesting… And extremely challenging to understand. Not only is everyone different, but when you're dating another person(s), you're exponentially making matters more difficult! Not only do you have to figure out your own ordeal, you have to blindly (that is, if you don't communicate well) figure out the other person's as well!

"Are they going to kiss me?"; "Do they *like* like me?"; "If they tell me they love me, do I have to reciprocate? Cause I really don't know…"; "Do they know I'm dating someone else?"; "Are they looking for something serious, or am I just a fling?"; "Are we exclusive, or not?"

Labeling… You eventually reach a certain period of your life when asking your lover the age-old question, "Will you be my girlfriend/boyfriend?" becomes very UNcool. But thanks to Facebook, now you can be even MORE childish, and report your relationship status to the world! And unreport… And report AGAIN! And unreport… What can I say?!? 'It's complicated…'

When you eventually find the one that you want to be socially and intimately linked to, and the two of you have reached the anxiety-evoking cross point of agreeing on the monogamous relationship, things should get as easy as bunny-slopping from then on out! At least for a little while…

You'll find yourselves enjoying each other's little quirks.

You'll begin to invent inside jokes, and you'll describe every little thing that your partner does as comical and sugary sweet. This is because when people are in a new relationship and surpass the simple feeling of lust, they start "falling in love". Although, this intense romance called "love" is not a simple emotion. It's much more complex than that. It's a goal-directed drive that helps the brain steer cognitive behavior. In other words, love is chemically driven and fucks with your brain!

People WANT to fall in love. Haven't you ever heard of people who are in love with falling in love? A lot of teenagers fall into this category. And there's a reason for that. Love fulfills people. So, depending on how unfulfilled one is, depends on how much they want another person to come into their lives and fulfill them! How does love fulfill someone? By mindfucking, of course!

For starters, when you're in an intimate relationship with someone, you experience more affection than when you are by yourself. This pertains to either an FWB, or a monogamous relationship, or even a polygamous relationship. The added affection draws out the hormone, oxytocin. Oxytocin is released in the hypothalamus and runs into our bloodstream. It makes us feel good. *Real good.* It also reduces stress levels, lowers blood pressure, increases tolerance for pain, and most importantly, improves our mood. This is JUST what the extra initial affection does to us.

Once *intense* romantic feelings begin to grow, people fall more into the entrapment of love. Certain receptors in the brain become activated. These receptors are linked to the neurotransmitters, dopamine and norepinephrine. And, these messengers are directly correlated to states of euphoria, obsession, addiction, and sleeplessness. Let's talk about sleeplessness… People who admit to being "in love" report thinking about their loved one eighty-five percent of their waking hours. Of course sleeplessness is going to happen! They need to steal those extra hours of sleep! How the hell else are they going to get anything done?!? Well, whether people who are "in love" are productive or not; when love prevails, their love-related neural networking system is definitely working overtime!

But these feelings of ecstasy wear off...

As time goes on, they'll begin to discover their lover's flaws. And what seemed to be tolerable at one time may slightly begin to get on their nerves-to put it politely. Depending on what age you are, and how experienced you are with relationships, you will make one of two decisions when you get to this roadblock: 1) You try to change the person, or 2) you ask yourself the question, "Can I deal with this for the rest of my life?"

Let's begin with number one, shall we? For those of you little ones, who think that you can change your man or woman... That's sweet. You are so young, and so pure... So, please excuse my bluntness: Your partner is not a dog. They may physically resemble a dog, but it takes an extremely talented animal trainer to train a man to stop looking at the women who walk past his view on the streets. It would be just as difficult training a woman to stop yappin' when gossip is abounding.

The truth about your relationship is that you CANNOT change the one you're with! If you're under the age of thirty, yes your partner will sooner or later endure the act of maturity. Perhaps they will learn to pick up their clothes, and wash the dishes. And if not, those simple tasks are trainable. But if you're expecting your partner to become more motivated, not lose their temper so quickly, or their family, you're screwed... Unfortunately, not literally...

You see, if your partner has things about them that you are unsatisfied with you have to analyze whether these traits are biological or psychological. Either way, again... You're screwed. The easiest way to investigate your partner's traits is to look at their family. They most likely are the way they are because they were trained by their family or simply inherited it from their family genetically. If that's the case, it's genetically ingrained in them...

In other words-UNTRAINABLE! And by the way? Almost every characteristic is genetically related… Even cheating! That's right! If you're a cheater, most likely you gained that from one of your parental figures. And they gained it from your sweet ol' Granny or Grandpa.

As for option number two, once you realize that your partner's shortcomings are unchangeable, the focus should be on you. Can you deal with these things? If not, this person's not right for you. Don't sell yourself short, either. If your loved one does shit that you don't deserve, but you stay with them because you don't think you could do better or because you don't have the energy to find an upgraded version, perhaps it is time for you to be by yourself for a little while.

For those of you who feel as though you "couldn't do better"-well, you're probably right… (Didn't expect that piece of advice, did ya?!) If you're with someone that you don't consider your "soulmate" perhaps you should get rid of them! But before you find someone new, first thing's first! You'll need to work on yourself! So, prioritize yourself; and when you are the best you can be, you'll be able to find someone that compliments you perfectly. I'm not saying that you should believe in 'love at first sight' and 'soulmates'; but, if you're in a relationship that doesn't make you deliriously happy (and I'm talking YEARS into it-not just the first six months during the brainwashing phase), than you may be with the wrong person. The sad part is that the majority of people who are unhappy with their relationship need to upgrade themselves before they upgrade their partner. And this is why so many people are in unhappy relationships. It's purely because they are too lazy and too unmotivated to better themselves. Most importantly, in order to better oneself, they sometimes have to take an inordinate amount of time being alone. And it's this alone time that scares them. So because the person that they're with accepts them and has created a comfortable lifestyle with them, they chose to remain committed to their current partner.

They choose to settle...

So rethink your relationship if you're in one. And if you're not happy, remember: It's not them... It's you. And if you're single searching for your one, true love-have fun shopping! And good luck!

References:

Bianchi-Demicheli, F., Grafton, S. T., & Ortigue, S. (2006). The power of love on the human brain. *Social Neuroscience*, 1(2), 90-130.

Erikson, E. (1950). *Childhood & Society*. Toronto: McLeod Limited.

National Institutes of Health. (2007). The Power of Love. Retrieved from http://newsinhealth.nih.gov

Tennov, D. (1979). *Love and limerence: The experience of being in love*. New York: Stein & Day.

Toscana, S. (2007). A grounded theory of female adolescents' dating experiences and factors influencing safety: The dynamics of the Circle. *BMC Nursing*, 6(7), 1-12.

THE FOUR RINGS

I, _____ , take you, _____ , to be my wedded
   your name here   *person of your choice*

_____ . To have and to _____ , from this day forward, for
   noun   *verb*

_____ , for _____ , for _____ , for _____ , in
 adjective   *adjective*   *adjective*   *adjective*

_____ or in _____ , to _____ and to _____
  verb   *verb*   *verb*   *transitive verb*

'till death do us part. And hereto I pledge you my _____ .
                                                         noun

No matter how you creatively fill in these marital libs, when
someone reads these vows aloud to their partner, family & friends,
and God, they are making a promise to legally attach themselves to
this person. Depending on your views and cultural background, the
meaning behind marriage can be as great as an eternal bond or as
simple as a piece of paper. Either way, you're attaching yourself to this
person for the rest of your life. Let me repeat: The rest of your life!!!

Engagement Ring: You, your boyfriend, and your friends are on
a rooftop drinking beers. He asks for everyone's attention, steps
up on the edge of the roof, and turns toward the crowd. "I have an
announcement," he yells. "I have had the privilege of being with
my girlfriend for five years now. I think it's time for me to pop the
question." He turns to his friend. "Mike, may I have the ring?" As

you crunch your hands over your beaming smile, you watch with wide eyes as Mike tosses the ring to your boyfriend. Unfortunately, the toss is a little wide, and as your boyfriend reaches out and grabs nothing but air, he loses his balance and falls three stories, to his untimely doom.

But no worries! Cause when you run to the edge of the roof to look over, expecting his body to be smashed all over the ground, you see him sinking slowly into an inflatable rescue mattress with a banner reading, "Will you marry me?" Exciting? Yes! Spontaneous? Yes! Did he really fall to his untimely doom? Well, depending on whom you ask, mayhaps. *I mean, he's not dead… But he is engaged…*

Planning a wedding is like having a second *or third* job. The engagement period is often rated as one of the happiest times in a person's life! (Unless you're asking a Maid of Honor. Then, it can possibly be rated as one of the worst times in their life.) Either way, it's a lot of hard work; especially, if your boss is a *Bridezilla*. The average time it takes someone to plan a wedding is fifteen months. So, Engagement Ring Takers: Remember that your number one goal during those fifteen months shouldn't be party planning. It should be glowing with pure joy and excitement. You and your partner have decided to take your relationship to the next level. Be happy, not stressed! As for all you Engagement Ring Givers: This step is a huge deal. As I wrote before, it is sometimes referred to as the happiest time in one's life! So, give your partner the true engagement they deserve. Research the ring before you get it (asking their BFF is always a plus), propose on a non-holiday (not on a day when they're EXPECTING something-it takes away from the spontaneity), and make the moment memorable (don't propose over the phone-who are you, Alexander Graham Bell?)

Wedding Ring: After a year and a half of crazy planning, your day finally arrives. Your drama-addicted bridesmaid is in tears, but you're ok. Your groom sees you before you even walk down the aisle, but that's ok! Red wine stains your bright white dress, but it's ok! Because you are marrying the man (or woman) of your dreams. Your best friend is now your spouse. It is the happiest day of your life since... Well... Since your last divorce!

When you choose to marry someone, you are choosing to take the leap. You are telling them that "they are the one", and there is no one else for you. You want to spend the rest of your life with that person. You want to grow together, possibly have a family, but most importantly, support and love one another for the rest of your lives. It is a beautiful thing if you find someone that you truly want to unite your life with. When they say, "It's better to have loved and lost than never to have loved at all," it's because you should consider yourself lucky when you experience giving true love-and actually receiving it in return. But unfortunately, life has its ups and downs. And it's not always golden skies. Sometimes it's more like *Golden Corral*...

SuffeRING: *Whoops!* You lose your job. Due to the past three excessive pregnancies, you haven't had a full night of sleep since you were blacked out in college. Your oldest kid is a fuck-up. Your spouse is drunk. The last time you had sex, you were still able to fit into your skinny jeans. (I'm not saying you looked *good* in them! I'm just saying you could fit *in* them.)

But it's ok, right? Cause you have your missing piece! And the two of you will be together through thick and thin! *Right?* Oh... Did I forget to mention that you're about to hit your mid-life crisis?

Seriously though... What happens when one person's life holds back another? What happens when depression hits one of you? What happens when one of you hits rock bottom? What happens when someone else comes into the picture? What happens when one of you gains weight and the other one loses attraction to you? It happens... All the time!

It's at this point, the question of divorce arises. Some people fear that word, while others desperately desire attaining it, more so than the desire of a starving zombie at a medical convention. It's a known fact that around 50% of marriages fail with divorce. But I'm happy to report that the lifespan of a marriage isn't as guileless as a coin toss. There are certain things you can do to lower your chances of getting a divorce. The factor like coming from parents who had a solid, loving relationship will definitely 'up' the chances of you having one yourself. But variables like that aren't under your control. However, there are some that you can take charge of!

For instance, if you get your college degree, you'll decrease the chance that you'll go through a divorce by 13%. *Why*? Well, isn't that the point of the whole book? If you put yourself first, before running into a marriage and/or kids, you'll be a much happier *and smarter* being! In fact, if you wait to get married until *after* the age of 25, you'll be 24% LESS likely to get a divorce. Remember, the brain doesn't fully develop until the age of thirty. So, you're even MORE safe if you wait until your forties. It may seem like a long time, but 40s are the new 20s these days, aren't they?

No worries if worse comes to worse though. I mean, yeah… You'll be wasting some years of your life, but you won't be alone. The average length of a marriage is ~8 years, and considering how many people are getting married to the wrong person at the wrong time, in our country divorce happens every 13 seconds. On a positive note, that's more often than a person getting killed in a car crash. And *exponentially* more frequent than a person getting bit by a shark! You may be thinking, *That's not actually a "positive" note.* But I don't know about you; I'd rather go through a divorce than die. So, I'm kind of diggin' the odds.

PerseveRING: In the case that you communicate well enough to move forward, have success by attending couples counseling, or are simply too lazy to separate, there is a chance for a positive outcome. And that's because if you stick it out for years to come, when you look back and reflect on your career, your family, your travels; you're most likely going to associate them with your spouse (cause they were there for a huge chunk of it). And amidst all of the crap that the two of you have endured, it's probable that you'll ultimately conclude that marrying them was the best decision you've *actually ever* made!

Or maybe not… But then again, whose fault is that?

Everyone aims for no regrets in life. And when you're head over heels for someone, it's almost impossible to fathom the day you'd rather take a cheese grater to your face then stay married to them. But behind all of this cynicism, there are strong, lifelong marriages. Yes, they DO EXIST! There are plenty of married couples who have successfully crossed the bridge from the suffering phase to the persevering phase, and guess what?!?! Their hard work paid off; they made it! And if the two of you can grow synchronously (or close enough) together, there's a huge chance that you will build a relationship based off of trust, partnership, forgiveness, love and laughter.

You see? There is a bright side to the four rings! Until recently, our culture was theoretically setting us up for failure. It was looked down upon to have sex before marriage-forcing people to get married earlier on, resulting in more divorces. It was frowned upon to move in with your lover before wearing a wedding band-forcing people to pay double the rent and rush into things too quickly. Finally, until recently it was illegal for same-sex couple to get married.

Some may say that our culture's morality is decreasing, but let me conclude this chapter with a case scenario: (Go back twenty years.) Joe is from an ethical, Christian family. He has been on the honor roll his entire life, was elected as the "Nicest Person" for his senior superlative, and has kept is sacred vow to his parents, church, and God-to hold off on sex until marriage. Joe is the spitting image of an ethical all-American boy. The problem is that as ethical and moral Joe tries to be, he's gay. And gay marriage isn't legal. What, is he supposed to die a virgin? Whether you're an advocate of gay marriage or not, you have to agree that *no* one deserves that!

…No one…

References:

Frosch, A. (2012, July 28). Interview by T. Puck [Email message to author]. Waiting.

Irvin, M. (2012). 32 Shocking Divorce Statistics. Retrieved from http://www.mckinleyirvin.com/blog/divorce/32-shocking-divorce-statistics/

Jaeger, C. (2012). Wedding Industry Statistics. Retrieved from http://weddingindustrystatistics.com/

Lemone, A. (2010). Interesting Engagement Statistics. Retrieved from http://ezinearticles.com/?Interesting-Engagement-Statistics&id=5529611

TheCalgarian1. "Crazy Marriage Proposal – Guy falls off building!!!" Online video clip. *YouTube*. Youtube, 11 July 2011. Web. 11 July 2013.

BETTER GET A KING!

The average human heart weighs around ten ounces. It is about the size of your fist. So, when someone says they love you with all of their heart, your response should be, "Is that it?" Visually, that's really not that impressive at all! In addition to the unsatisfaction that you may feel when someone expresses this metaphor to describe their love for you, you may feel a bit confused. *If you love me with all of your heart, how do you have any left over to love others? Are you just reusing the love? I mean, I'm an environmentalist and all, but I'm not into being on the receiving end of your "fungible" love. It doesn't seem to carry on as much weight as the non-recyclable kind.* Well, these questions and concerns don't come up when polyamorous people claim to love one another. They have more than enough love to go around, so I guess it's safe to say that the average polyamorous person *must* have a larger heart; and therefore, must be more useful in a fist-fight.

America is a monogamous country; although, there are over one hundred thousand people in the United States who practice polygamy. Certain "marriages" that fall under polygamy are: Polyandry, when a woman takes on multiple husbands; polygyny, when a man takes on multiple wives; and group marriage, which is when multiple people consider themselves "married" to each other. Legally, in this country, you're not able to be married to more than one person, which is probably a good thing; because to me, a cluster marriage sounds like nothing more than a cluster fuck! But that still doesn't stop people from being on the lookout for multiple loves or sex partners. And those Mormons... Well, let's just say if you're interested in circumnavigating a law, you can always do what Joseph Smith did and create your own religion. Dum, dum, dum, dum, dum...

There are a variety of polygamous relationships. The ones you're used to hearing about are probably the lifestyle of your slutty older sister who is currently juggling three guys at once, your bisexual friend who is randomly having sexual relations with a girl and a guy on separate occasions because she can't figure out which one she likes better, those old, married couples who partake in swinging activities and your best friend, the BJ King, who gets a different knobber every weekend. All of the polygamous examples above are purely pleasure-driven. But there is a responsible, non-monogamous sexual relationship that people call polyamory.

Polyamory isn't just an excuse that you can use to validate last night's cheating extravaganza to your girlfriend. It's a way of life that is very hard for the average American to comprehend. Polyamory means "many loves". It is not a cult, and it is not a sexual orientation. It is simply a lifestyle, or way of living. A polyamourous relationship involves an intertwined group of people who have loving and intimate relationships with each other. Although it is not associated with any specific type of sexual identity, it does consist of a lot of bisexual and 'heteroflexible' people.

Polyamory is not bisexuality; although, the two are subjected to similar judgment. Even though the gay community appears accepting of all sexual orientations, even some of them do not support the idea of bisexuality. Sorry people! But sexuality is not mathematics. There is no right or wrong answer. The answer to someone's sexual orientation lies within how they feel at that moment; and is ever-changing. As for discrimination with polyamory; many monogamous people in the United States cannot comprehend the idea of polyamory. They feel as though you're either polygamous or monogamous-there is no such thing as being monogamous in a polygamous relationship. But there is!

There are plenty of successful polyamorous relationships that exist. These cellular families may include a delta, a quad, and even more sided figures!! You may be thinking, *Wow! These households must have raging orgies going on all day long!* But it's not like that at all. The relationships that these members have with each other are just as uninterestingly normal as some monogamous relationships. In addition, not everyone in the family has a sexual relationship with each and every member. It is a loving and open group, but depending on the personalities and sexual orientations of each member, determines who develops a sexual relationship with whom. Some may say two's company, three's a crowd, four's a party; but others may argue, "The more people, the more complicated..."

To avoid complications, members of the family, or relationship, create a list of 'house rules'. In order for these rules to work, everyone must be honest at the time of creating the rules, to reduce any stressful issues. One of the most important rules that is usually created in a poly relationship is honesty. This is usually followed by respect, then communication. Funny how these rules seem like the most important in any relationship! That's because a polyamourous relationship isn't much different than a "normal" monogamous relationship! (Here's your "ah-ha" moment...)

Why would someone choose to be in a polyamorous relationship? Well, people who are in a relationship with another person sometimes expect that their significant other is always going to fill the necessary gaps in their life and give them the feeling of being complete. Realistically, that's a lot to ask from your partner. If you have the loving capacity to open up your relationship and share intimacy, sexual experiences, and friendship with multiple people, the chances are higher that you'll ultimately feel more fulfilled. When one is honestly able to view multiple loves as a positive, they experience actual joy from seeing their partner receive pleasure from another person. This feeling, called compersion, is the opposite of jealousy and is extremely liberating for those who truly sense it.

Why would someone choose not to be in a polyamorous relationship? If someone is deeply rooted from a monogamous family, and values and enjoys being in a monogamous relationship, polyamory is probably not for them. Another type of person who would probably have an unsuccessful poly relationship would be someone who has a problem with jealousy. Me personally? I grew up with three older brothers… I don't share. But if you are curious to explore your sexual chi, and interested in finding some new relational energy, feel free to *GTS*! One reputable, nationwide polyamory organization that provides a plethora of communal activities for poly people and supporters is *Loving More*.

You may be thinking, *I don't think I'd be able to share my wife, but I would like to cheat on her every once in a while!* Well, that's plain and simple adultery, my Friend. But if you'd be open to cheating together with your wife, maybe swinging can be your thing! Swinging is when you and your partner have a mutual agreement to engage in sexual relations with other people. It usually happens at the same time in the same place. The majority of swingers are highly educated, middle class young adults in their twenties and thirties. Swingers are very sociable people who are known to have liberal views on sexuality, non-sexual topics and politics as well! It's not that these people do not value their monogamous relationship. They are just able to alter the rules to have a little extra fun! Don't think of the fact that these people can willingly cheat on each other and go back to having a loving marriage the next day labels them as having an unhealthy relationship. A study actually revealed that couples who are involved in swinging seek less mental health professionals than people who aren't. So, perhaps their cheating ways are their key to a happy and healthy relationship! Either way, polygamy is not for everyone, but as you grow as an individual and as a partner in a long-term relationship, your views on monogamy can sometimes change. So, remember to openly communicate your interests with your partner and maybe one day you will find yourself in a sloppy, chocolatey orgy at an adult buffet.

When queen-size beds suddenly feel too small... Experiencing sex with multiple partners can be great fun! Although it makes it more difficult to choose the toppings on the pizza you're going to order afterwards; if the pizza delivery man is hot enough, there may be no objection from anyone in your party if you want to ask him to stay and play! And when you call out the wrong name in bed, it JUST doesn't seem so bad... (Cause it's probably the person to your left.)

Yes, enjoying intercourse and oral sex simultaneously is almost as great as naked *Twister* (which it kind of already is); just remember, while fore-playing with four players, to always practice safe sex. Sure, people in *Walgreens* may give you a funny look when you go out comparison shopping for condoms; but, it's always better and safer to have each and every dick perfectly TayloRed to. In case you are in fear of contracting an STI when experimenting with multiple partners, don't be pressured to share bodily fluids with everyone. Body fluid monogamy is completely acceptable, and to reduce your concern for safety, create a protection contract for all involved parties. Whether you use dental dams or condoms, make it known: It's not about who you fuck or what you fuck, but that you fuck... Safely. (Did you write that down?)

References:

Fang, B. (1976). Swinging: In retrospect. *The Journal of Sex Research*, 12(3), 220-237.

Gilmartin, B. G. (1975). That swinging couple down the block. *Psychology Today*, 8, 54-58.

Klesse, C. (2006). Polyamory and its 'Others': Contesting the terms of non-monogramy. *Sexualities*, 9(5), 565-583.

Parker, T. (Writer & Director). (2003). All about Mormons [Television series episode]. In T. Parker& M. Stone (Producers), *South Park*. United States: Comedy Central.

Schwartz, F. (2012, August 20). Interview by T. Puck [Phone conversation]. Polyamory, Widener University.

Walshok, M. L. (1971). The emergence of middle-class deviant subcultures: The case of swingers. *Social Problems*, 18, 488-495.

Xeromag. (2012). Polyamory glossery. Retrieved from http://www.xeromag.com/fvpolyglossary.html

WHO THE FUCK IS TAYLOR PUCK?

TayloR Puck is a dating sexpert and trained sex educator. She has a bachelor's degree in biology and psychology, a master's degree in science education, and a master's degree in human sexuality. TayloR attends Widener University and is in the process of earning her doctorate in human sexuality.

TayloR spent most of her twenties as an educator in public high schools and colleges, but decided to break away from the conventional education system in hopes to make more of an impact on young adults. Today, she devotes her time to writing and researching. As a sexologist, TayloR educates people while entertaining them with her comical narratives. She strives to give adults of all ages the sexual education they **truly want** and **need** to know. TayloR's goal is to diminish the stigma that America places on sexuality, as well as promote fun and safe sex!

TayloR lives in New York City. In her spare time, when taking a break from her chronic dating schedule, she can be found hiking with her two Jack Russell Terriers. As an outdoor enthusiast, TayloR spends her free time snowboarding, surfing or drinking margaritas on Florida beaches. She is known for her positive energy, sense of humor, extreme bluntness and romantic conquests.

INDEX

-A-
Abortifacient 31
Abortion 26, 31, 33, 34
Abortion Pill (see 'Medical abortion')
Abstinence 26, 27, 37
Abstinence-only (education) 12, 14
Acne 20
Addiction 204
Age of legal consent 189
AIDS (Acquired Immune Deficiency
     Syndrome) 41, 42
Alzheimer's disease 106
Ambiguous genitalia 56, 57, 58, 59
Androgen 53, 67
Androgynous 84, 85
Asexual 66, 143
Asphyxiaphilic 124

-B-
Basal body temperature 31, 32
Bath salts 109
BDSM 124, 126, 128, 129
Bear 71
Bestiality 171-175
Birth control 25-36
Bisexual 64, 66, 67, 75, 76, 216
Blastocyst 19
Blow job (BJ) 12, 105, 116, 173, 179, 216
Body image 20, 91-100, 108, 134, 152
Bondage 20, 124
Breast 21, 75, 77, 79, 92, 106, 107, 117
Breastfeeding 107, 121
Bullying 69, 70, 167

-C-
Calendar method 31
CD4 41
Cervical cap 30
Cervical os 31
Chlamydia 40, 44
Circles of Sexuality 16
Cirrhosis 42
Clitoridectomy 119
Clitoris 21, 56, 117, 119, 135, 143
Comprehensive sex (education) 12, 14, 16
Condom 15, 29, 33, 37, 38, 39, 40, 42, 44,
     47, 106, 117, 118, 185, 186, 188, 199,
     201, 219
Consensual sex 173, 190
Contraception 15, 25, 26, 27, 31, 33, 34
Cortisol 134
Crabs 45, 46
Cross dresser 81

-D-
Date drug 188
Depo (Depo-Provera) 28
Diaphragm 29, 30
Discipline 124
Dopamine 126, 149, 204
Down syndrome 55

-E-
Eating disorder 93
Ecstasy (MDMA) 108, 109, 189
Egg Production 27
Ejaculation 34, 35, 118, 133
Embryo 19, 54
Emergency contraception 33
Endorphins 127
Erogenous zone 107, 134
Estrogen 27, 28, 53
Exhibitionism 125, 127, 168

-F-
Fantasy 123-130, 151
Fellatio 65
Female condom 29
Fertility Awareness-Based Methods (FAB)
     31-33
Fertilization 31, 58
Fetus 19, 54
Flirtation 155-163, 166
Friends with benefits 142, 198, 199, 200,
     204

-G-
Gay 63, 64, 66, 67, 68, 69, 70, 71, 75, 76, 78,
     86, 144, 168, 191, 192, 213, 216
Gender 20, 64, 75, 76, 77, 78, 79, 80, 83,
     84, 86, 87, 91, 119, 125, 148, 157, 191
Gender Identity Disorder (GID) 77
Gender roles 83-87, 148
Genitals 20, 56, 57, 59, 60, 78, 113, 119,

135, 143, 179
Genotype 53
Gonorrhea 40, 44, 45
Gynecomastia 20

-H-
Hepatitis 40
Hermaphrodite 56
Herpes 40, 43, 44
Heteronormality 67
Heterosexuality 64, 67
HIV (Human Immunodeficiency Virus) 15,
    31, 40, 41, 42, 45
Homophobia 70, 71
Homosexuality 63, 70, 71
Hook up 197-201
HPV (Human Papilloma Virus) 40, 43
H-Y antigen 54

-I-
Incest 107, 177-180
Indifferent gonads 54
Intercourse 113, 198, 219
Intersex 56, 57, 60
IUD (Intrauterine device) 31

-K-
Kama Sutra 131-135
Karyotypes 56
Kinsey Scale 64, 65
Kit Kat (Ketamine) 189
Klinefelter syndrome 55

-L-
Labia majora 117
Labia minora 117
Lesbian 72, 75, 76, 78, 84, 124
Levonorgestrel 33
LGBTQ 75, 175
Lipstick lesbians 72
Liquid Ecstasy (GHB) 189

-M-
Marriage 178, 179, 198, 201, 209-213, 215,
    216, 218
Masochism 43, 109, 124, 127
Masturbation 98, 113, 142, 174
Medical abortion 34
Menarche 13, 21

Menstrual Cycle 27, 32, 57
Menstruation 27, 32, 33, 117
Mexican Valium (Rohypnol) 189
Monogamy 219
Mullerian System 54

-N-
Napoleon Complex 94
Nipples 116, 127
Noonen syndrome 55
Norepinephrine 204
NuvaRing 28

-O-
Oedipus Complex 70
Oral sex 37, 219
Orgasm 20, 21, 78, 83, 86, 113, 115, 118-
    121, 132, 133, 135, 136, 172, 183, 200
Os (See 'Cervical os')
Ovaries 53, 54
Ovulation 27, 28, 31-34, 57, 141
Ovulation method 31, 33
Oxytocin 121, 204

-P-
Paraphilia 128
Patch (Ortho Evra) 28
Penis 29, 35, 38, 39, 53, 55, 56, 68, 117,
    118, 131, 134, 135, 171, 173
Phenotype 179
Pill 27, 28, 33, 34, 77, 108
Plan B 33, 34
Plateau 115, 117
PMS 27
Polyamory 216-218
Polygamy 215, 218
Pornography 13, 65, 66, 91, 125, 128,
    150-152, 166
Pregnancy 28, 29, 117
Progestin 28, 31
Psychosomatic circle of sex 113, 119
Puberty 13, 20-22, 26, 55, 79
Puberty blockers 79
Pubic lice (see 'Crabs')

-Q-
Queer 75, 76, 78

-R-

Rape (Spousal, gang, date, prison) 116, 125, 126, 129, 142, 178, 183-193
Reproductive system 31
Resolution 115, 120
RU-486 (see 'Medical abortion')

-S-

Sadism 124
Seduction 126, 127
Seminal vesicles 54
Sensate Focus 131-133
Serotonin 108, 109
Sex change (see sex reassignment surgery, gender affirming surgery**)
Sex chromosomes 55, 56
Sex flush 116-118
Sex roles 83, 84
Sexting 167, 168
Sexual deviations 173
Sexual dysfunction 13, 114, 132, 133, 143
Sexual harassment 165-167, 169
Sexual orientation 15, 16, 20, 64, 66, 67, 69-72, 76-78, 84, 148, 175, 216, 217
Sexual perversions 173
Sexual response cycle 113-115, 121
Skin hunger 104, 106, 107-110
Social learning theory 150, 151
Sperm 11, 19-21, 26, 29-32, 34, 35, 54, 57, 118
Spermicide 30, 31
Sponge 30
SRY gene 54
Statutory rape 189, 190
STDs (see STIs)
STIs 26, 29, 38-47
Stock market orgasm 136
'Super' Gonorrhea 45
Surgical abortion 33, 34
Swinging 135, 216, 218
Syphilis 44, 45

-T-

T cell 41
Tantra 131-133
Tantric orgasm 136
Testes 54, 117
Testicals 55, 117, 127, 141
Testosterone 21, 54, 77
Transgender 75-80
Transsexual 77, 79
Trichomoniasis 46
Trisomy 13 (Patau syndrome) 55
Trisomy 18 (Edwards syndrome) 55
Tubal ligations (see 'Tying of the tubes')
Turner syndrome (XO) 55
Tying of the tubes 35

-U-

Uterus 29-31, 34, 54, 118

-V-

Vagina 19, 21, 28-33, 39, 41, 54, 56, 57, 117, 118, 141
Vas deferens 35, 54
Vasectomy 35
Vibrator 21, 86
Voyeurism 125, 127, 128, 151
Vulva 53, 56

-W-

Westermarck Hypothesis 179
Wet dream 21
Withdraw 34, 38
Wolffian System 54

-X-

X chromosome 54-56

-Y-

Y chromosome 54, 56

-Z-

Zoophilia 174
Zoosexual 175
Zygote 19